WE SAILED
IT OUR WAY

VALERIE AND NEIL MCBROOM

WE SAILED IT OUR WAY

Valerie McBroom and Neil McBroom

SPORTS & RECREATION / Sailing

TRAVEL / Essays & Travelogues

BIOGRAPHY & AUTOBIOGRAPHY / Sports

 £16.99   9781398402041

 £3.50   9781398402058

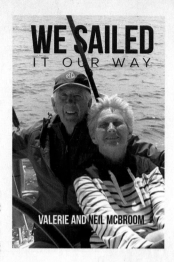

This story is about two people, born into the uncertainties of the 1939–1945 War, who fell in love with each other and with sailing and who, encouraged by the example of other seafarers, completed over a period of 50 years a circumnavigation of the world's favourite sailing destinations albeit missing out the long blue bits.

The book contains anecdotes as well as practical advice ensuring it is a must-read for boat lovers as well as those yet to find their sea legs. There is seamanship on every page. It will have a special appeal for those contemplating sailing in distant waters who wish to compare cruising grounds.

As well as covering sailing and seamanship, it is a travelogue in its own right, reflecting the history and culture met along the way.

--✂------

Please send me ...... copy/ies of

We Sailed It Our Way

Valerie McBroom and Neil McBroom

Please add the following postage per book:
United Kingdom £3.00 / Europe £7.50 /
Rest of World £12.00

Delivery and Payment Details

Format	Price	Qty	Total
Paperback ☐			
Subtotal			
Postage			
Total			

Full name: ....

Street Address ....

City:.. County:...

Postcode: .... Country: ....

Phone number (inc. area code): .... Email: ....

I enclose a cheque for £.................. payable to Austin Macauley Publishers LTD.

Please send to: Austin Macauley, CGC-33-01, 25 Canada Square, Canary Wharf, London E14 5LQ

Tel: +44 (0) 207 038 8212
Fax: +44 (0) 207 038 8100
orders@austinmacauley.com
www.austinmacauley.com

AUSTIN MACAULEY PUBLISHERS™
LONDON • CAMBRIDGE • NEW YORK • SHARJAH

Born in 1939, Neil McBroom was educated at King Edwards School, Birmingham, where his sailing interest was founded. He met Valerie McBroom at College in London where he read Metallurgy and Valerie Mathematics. They married in 1966. By this time, Neil had attended Outward Bound and was invited back as Instructor. This led to berths as a Watch Officer on the "Sir Winston Churchill" and "Malcolm Miller". Their Odyssey began with UK charters and moved on to flotilla holidays and far flung bare boat charters. Both had published papers so the confidence existed to write about their experiences. Their sailing legacy has been passed to their two daughters and four grandchildren.

Authors' Note

It is hoped this book will appeal to both sailors and travellers alike. It sets out to be more than a travelogue, since travelling combined with sailing provides experience over and above the norm. Sailing promises adventure and discovery. More than this it promotes self-discovery. This is particularly the case for younger sailors who get involved in character forming adventures.

It has proved a worthwhile project for the authors since it provides an opportunity for us to pay tribute to the various people, organisations and venues that have made it possible. We can also recognise the contribution played by friends and family who have made the journey with us.

Neil would like, in particular, to recognise the contribution made to his life by Outward Bound, the Sail Training Association and King Edward's School, Birmingham.

Valerie and Neil McBroom

WE SAILED IT OUR WAY

AUSTIN MACAULEY PUBLISHERS™

LONDON ∗ CAMBRIDGE ∗ NEW YORK ∗ SHARJAH

A CIP catalogue record for this title is available from the British Library.

ISBN 9781398402041 (Paperback)
ISBN 9781398402058 (ePub e-book)

www.austinmacauley.com

First Published (2021)
Austin Macauley Publishers Ltd
25 Canada Square
Canary Wharf
London
E14 5LQ

Table of Contents

Our Early Days

I was born in 1939 and Valerie in 1942, not auspicious times to come into the World. Our early lives were shaped by the impact of the 1939-45 war on our parents.

In Valerie's case, her father served in the Royal Artillery, first in Europe and later in Palestine. He kept a meticulous diary of his life with revealing comments such as 'slept in a bed' and 'rumours that Cologne has fallen'. He came out unscathed and returned to the family business but with young years wasted. In later life he had to cope with a serious motor cycle accident to Valerie's brother and with the ill health and premature death of Valerie's mother. Valerie also had a tough time; she was evacuated away from home into the care of Uncles and Aunts and for some time after her father's return, he was "Uncle Daddy". The jewel in the crown of her early life was her education at Streatham and Clapham High School, part of the Girls Public Day School Trust.

I had similar issues. The family lived in Small Heath, Birmingham, close to the BSA (Birmingham Small Arms) factory where GP father ran a first aid post, an experience which destroyed his health and left his wife distraught. Again, education saved the day. I with my brother had been "prepared" (West House School) for entry to Public School but I managed a scholarship to King Edwards School. My sister was at KES Girls School following her return from evacuation in Scotland and my brother attended Malvern College.

Education was at the core of our young lives. Valerie and I both wound up as children of Harold Wilson's "White Hot Technological Revolution" which involved studying for a BSc. at the emerging Colleges of Advanced Technology, in our case Battersea, which eventually morphed into Universities. We were delighted years later to receive Honorary Degrees from Surrey University. Valerie was in the van of technology change; as a student she worked on computer programs to feed fuel rods to the Sizewell reactor and also to optimise British Oxygen's distribution of gas bottles. Meanwhile, I was boning up on the business of steelmaking in Ebbw Vale and Newport where a pair of rugby boots came in handy.

Then we got married and we set up home in Wolverhampton since I was now at the GKN Research Laboratories and Valerie was optimising yield in the nearby Tube Investments Plant. Our two children, Moira and Fiona, were born in Wolverhampton. With Moira, I just managed to return from a GKN assignment in Calcutta to find Valerie was being confined at the RAF Hospital at Cosworth as at that time no maternity hospital was available in Wolverhampton. I was advised by phone in the middle of the night that I now had a baby daughter; when I rang the hospital the next morning, they informed me my baby son was fine! It got sorted. Fiona's arrival was more straightforward.

After a stint in a Rolling Mill in North Cheshire, in 1976 we moved to Cardiff, our adopted and much-loved City. Here our family grew up, were schooled, chose their careers, got married and disappeared back across the borders to build their own lives. However, it was from Cardiff, with the proximity of Pembrokeshire, where our Sailing Odyssey took wing. First let's look at some key building blocks.

Outward Bound

In my last year at School, I was fortunate to be sent to the Outward Bound School at Aberdovey. Outward Bound was set up in 1942 by Lawrence Holt of the Blue Funnel Line and expatriate German Kurt Hahn. Kahn was also responsible for establishing Gordonstoun, Atlantic College and the Duke of Edinburgh Award Scheme. In 1942, Britain was not only losing ships but she was losing sailors who had not been trained to be proactive in adversity. Outward Bound with its mission statement of 'to serve, to strive and not to yield' aimed, by means of exposing youngsters to circumstances which require self-discipline and teamwork, to transform defeatist attitudes into positive attitudes, not just under hardship but also in life generally.

With sailing experience gained on School Norfolk Broads trips and being at school used to organising younger boys, I was appointed leader of my watch. I was further fortunate in that the appointed Watch Officer was from the RAF with no real sailing experience which meant I shouldered much of the responsibility. We sailed heavy 32' dipping lug cutters where the gaff of the foresail had to be dipped round the mast on every tack (passing through the wind). The first day out in a fresh wind, I could see boats ahead were failing to tack through the wind, a problem common on Broads boats. Instead of tacking, we wore round (turned downwind through 270 degrees) and sailed smugly home on the other tack. Other duties followed which meant I was readily accepted as a Watch Officer when I later applied. I enjoyed the Watch Officer experience and felt a special empathy with my watch. In these early days of Outward Bound, many of the course members were from Approved Schools. It staggers me that it costs more now to keep a young offender in an Approved School or other Institution for a month than it does to send them to an Outward Bound School.

(While I was with GKN, there was a main board director called Oscar Hahn who was a nephew of Kurt Hahn. Oscar Hahn had polio in his youth and was confined to a wheelchair. From time to time you would be called before him to be upbraided for some sin; he used to bark at you and wave his stick. It was rumoured that on a visit to an electric furnace, an artificial leg had heated up and he'd had to leave in a hurry).

Being a temporary Watch Officer was also a stimulating experience but in a sense being an Officer in someone else's Ward Room, you are never completely at home. Also, I had as many mountain responsibilities as I did from sailing since I had earlier taken out Duke of Edinburgh parties. However, seeing the concepts of 'to serve, to strive and not to yield' instilled in youngsters was a rewarding experience. The major benefit to me was that my having served as a Watch Officer with Outward Bound, I was readily accepted for a berth as a Watch Office on the STA Schooners "Sir Winston Churchill" and "Malcolm Miller".

Tall Ships

It was both an enormous privilege and an exciting adventure to sail on these two ships. It was also a privilege to sail with the Masters and Mates who together with the other regular crew were quite literally keeping the UK's seamanship traditions alive. As I look out now on the tall ships' scene in the UK, it is depressing. The "Sir Winston Churchill" and the "Malcolm Miller" have been sold and converted into yachts. The latter was built by Sir James Miller, a former Lord Mayor of London and Lord Provost of Edinburgh, and named after Sir James's son Malcolm, who had been killed in a car accident. At the time of writing, The Ocean Youth Trust, spawned out of the Sail Training Association, has been forced to sell the brig "Prince William" and her sister ship "Stavros Niarchos". The only body which is weathering the economic storm of maintaining such vessels is the Jubilee Trust whose vessels "Lord Nelson" and "Tenacious" with their facilities for the disabled attract good support from the public.

The facilities aboard the barques "Lord Nelson" and "Tenacious", many of which were tried out and proved on a vessel called the "Soren Larsen", are worthy of mention. Sailors don't like holes in the deck and usually surround a hatch with a combing; to get a wheel chair hoist flush with the deck required a special approach. Other disabled features include a wheel chair ramp extending out along the bowsprit, access holes in the mast platforms to enable wheelchairs to be hoisted through and braille marks on the pin rails indicating the purpose of secured lines. One feature of the "Tenacious" which is unusual in a modern vessel of her size is that she has a wooden hull.

Another tall ship struggling to survive is the "Jeannie Johnston", a reproduction of an Irish Coffin ship involved in the migration of desperate Irish families from the potato famine. You have to visit Boston to fully appreciate the drama of these events. Apparently, young pregnant women were jumping into the freezing water since the authorities would not let them land. Meanwhile you had English landlords growing grain in Ireland for export into Europe. The "Jeannie Johnston" is currently moored in the River Liffey in Dublin, upriver from the cable stayed bridge, and is used as a conference centre.

Valerie and I have a personal interest in these times since it is possible that "McBroom" is a distortion of "O'Brien". My antecedents were either coalminers in the Ayrshire Coalfield (men) or web-offsetters in the textile mills of Kilmarnock (women), common sanctuaries for Irish migrants. My grandfather rose to be a collier manager and was able to ensure his issue were educated.

Amongst the most memorable of the regular crews on these vessels was Ken Groom; he served as mate in the "Sir Winston Churchill". His party piece was to slide down from the rigging with a shroud clasped between his feet and his hands cupped round the shroud. Captain Kemmis-Betty, also from the "Churchill", had a manner to match his name. He was the epitome of calmness and dignity in carrying out his duties. I remember one night when I had the morning watch. The standing orders stated '0200hrs tack ship'. Just before 2 am I went down to the saloon and the "old man" was dosing in a chair. I politely advised we were approaching 0200hrs. and we needed to tack. To my total astonishment, he replied, 'Mr McBroom, tack the ship.' Tacking the ship meant getting the off duty watch on deck, tensioning the leeward shrouds to take the strain as we tacked while at the same time loosening off those to windward (all heavy gear), tending to the never ending length of 3 headsheets which needed freed off and then re-tensioned and finally, heart in mouth, turning the wheel. I coped! It stands as one of the most memorable experiences of my life.

Sailing tall ships is not without its dangers. Quite recently a young cadet aboard the Sea Cadet's vessel "Royalist" fell from the rigging and lost his life. The Irish Sail Training vessel "Asgard II", as pretty a ship as ever you will find, sank off the coast of Brittany, not under press of weather but her engine room flooded after colliding with an object below the surface. In 2013, the Dutch training ship "Astrid" was driven on to rocks off Cork in Southern Ireland.

My most dangerous encounter was a collision between the "Miller" and the "Churchill". The Masters of the STA have a duty to show the ships in the best light. The "Churchill" and the "Miller" were on a parallel broad reach when the Brittany Ferry hove into view. The master of the "Miller" turned down wind to make a pass under the stern of the "Churchill". Unfortunately, he misjudged his pass and clipped the stern of the "Churchill" and damaged the bowsprit of the "Miller".

Bucking the trend away from conventional sail training ships was the modernisation in 1997 of the clipper "Pelican of London". Considerable research went into the redesign and reconstruction of this vessel including miniature models with different sail plans. Emerging from this work was the conclusion that a mast bearing square sails is best positioned between a fore and aft rigged foremast and a fore and aft rigged mizzen. This design flies in the face of traditional thinking and there will be considerable interest in how successful she is in the field of character development through sail training.

Neil a-top the mast on the "Sir Winston Churchill"

"Sir Winston Churchill"

Damaged bowsprit on "Malcom Miller"

Boys' Toys

The relative freedom of younger years coupled with a sense of adventure and a growing sailing experience are all catalysts for young men and increasingly so for young women, to sail off to the next adventure and the next challenge.

In my own case, I undertook a series of charter voyages with friends and colleagues, all of whom were prepared, (misguidedly!), to sail with me. The charters assumed a lot of names according to the source of the crews. We had the Wolverhampton Junior Chamber of Commerce crew, the Old Edwardians crew, the British Standards for Tool Steels crew, the GKN crew and even a crew of quite respectable bar flies and beach bums. I will leave to those who came and are reading this to decide in which crew they sailed! These cruises visited the Solent, the Isle of Mull in Scotland and made a Channel Crossing.

This was at a time that chartering was taking off and an article I wrote on our experiences was readily printed in Yachting Monthly (see Y.M., July 1976, Volume 136, No 840, p1028).

Inevitably in the early years, sailors can be challenged by events calling on a level of experience not yet met – therein lies the adventure. In my own case and looking back, we did have some hairy moments.

On one occasion, we were tacking out of Yarmouth (I.O.W.) against the flood and put the helm over just south of a port hand mark which consisted of a wooden tower. With wind and tide against us, we failed to make the tack and were in danger of being carried down on to the tower. Events such as these call for instant decisions with little regard to the consequences. Hence I wore round outside the channel marker to go back into the channel upstream. We waited with bated breath for the keel to take the ground but mercifully at mid-tide we didn't find it.

Another incident I recall was approaching Cherbourg in a fog. This was in the days before satellite navigation; instead you approached the harbour following a narrow radio signal on a specific bearing emanating from the entrance. We found the bearing in the fog and were steering down it. I was below when there was a shout from the cockpit, 'You'd better come up as a block of flats has appeared.' This of course was the Brittany Ferry doing the same thing as we were doing. It was a classic occurrence of that which you are warned about in all the manuals. The ferry overtook us and we no longer had to monitor the bearing, we just followed 'the block of flats'. Looking back, following someone else on the assumption that he has got it right is not full proof seamanship.

While we were in Cherbourg, we visited the fuel dock and it was not untypical of those early days that there ensued a vigorous discussion as to whether to fill up with diesel or petrol.

At about the same time of these early charters, I crewed for a local doctor who was relocating his boat from Cardiff to Milford Haven. This was the opposite of a no-brainer. Believe it or not, the rise and fall in Cardiff Bay is some 14 metres, second only to the Bay of Fundy in Newfoundland. In the Bristol Channel you don't so much as go for a sail but you sail about on a patch of water which is ebbing and flooding at a rate, more often than not, faster than you can sail. Even in Milford Haven you are still looking at a rise and fall of some 5 metres; bilge keels come in very handy as do cards and books while you take the ground and await the next flood. Cutting a long story short we were tacking into Limpert Bay towards Aberthaw Power Station with the echo sounder on and yet there was a considerable bang as our keel had an acquaintance with a rock. We had a rude wake-up call albeit without mishap and this in a boat where we considered we had local knowledge. Prudence is everything.

.

Boat Ownership

To have or not to have, that is the question. Whether it is nobler in the mind to suffer the slings and arrows of outrageous fortune associated with boat ownership or to take revenge against the inevitable sea of troubles generated and sail in someone else's boat or charter a boat. Ownership can often be a poisoned chalice, a source once said it's like standing in a cold shower tearing up £5 notes.

Yet the longing becomes irresistible. It is a subject which needs a cool head and a focussed mind. I regret that your scribe's approach initially was anything but that, more like chasing a "dream" which was far from focussed. The first approach was constrained by what boat could fit on the roof of a Ford Anglia. This turned out to be a very light plywood lug sailed "vessel", it hardly merited the title of "boat". We only sailed it once in the course of which it capsized under the bridge at Shillingford-on-Thames pitching my non sailing sister-in-law into the water.

The next foray into ownership was the sensible purchase of a GP14 complete with trailer. The objective was to sail this at the South Staffordshire Sailing Club based at a reservoir just north of Wolverhampton. However, the project had to compete with the presence of a new job, a new home and eventually the arrival of two children. During this period, I also spent a year as President of the Wolverhampton Junior Chamber of Commerce, a worthy institution which focussed more on "locals" than it did on local issues. Hence the GP was little used despite encouragement from work colleagues. However, it did have one excursion, coming with us on holiday in the Isle of Wight. Our first attempt to launch it failed due to the roughness of the incoming waves. Next day, a launch was successful and I set off for a good sail. Then, Valerie, relaxing on the beach, was awakened by a nearby cry, 'Oh look, that boat has capsized,' She sat up to see me frantically bailing out! We didn't try again!

On our move to Cheshire, the GP14 was sold but replaced by an Enterprise on the basis that both Lyme Park and Windermere were close by. It's funny how you can persuade yourself to suit a purpose. However, we did use the Enterprise and we have a delightful picture of younger daughter Fiona sitting bolt upright in a stiff lifejacket on the centreboard case fast asleep.

Then came the move to Cardiff as GKN's Chief Metallurgist and the priority of new responsibilities and a new environment. I have already dealt with the shortcomings of the estuary off Cardiff. Having made that point, the Cardiff Bay Shoreside Development has produced a usefully sized inland lake, within a barrier served by locks, for cruiser and dinghy sailing and berthing. The area is large enough to attract the contemporary Extreme Sailing Series with large catamarans flying a hull and occasionally, as captured on film, one of them flying both hulls.

There were other leisure priorities and the first of these was to establish a caravan on a site near to Dale, in the Milford Haven estuary. Dale is as snug and picturesque an anchorage as you can find. If it has a drawback, it is slightly cut off from routes to Pembrokeshire's other attractions and also contains some commerce in the form of fishing and leisure craft. This can give rise to mooring issues and we had our share over the years. Also, the Club House is not as thriving as say at the Newport (Pembs) Club. Having said that and with RYA involvement, the encouragement given to youngsters has been exemplary.

So began a long association as our children grew up. As part of this process, the Enterprise was replaced with a Mirror and a Sailboard. Suffice it to say that in later life, we continued to race the Mirror in the Dale Sailing Club Sunday morning race into our late sixties. We were a pain to the Starter. While the crews of the new classes of highly tuned dinghies were already in the "Griffin" pub, we were still out on the water.

Then on to Cruisers and the acquisition of "Moonfleet" our fondness for which eclipse the memories of prouder and more far flung craft. She was a Snapdragon 26 which provided a snug and traditional accommodation and a rig which was balanced and appropriate for her stubby bilge keels. For her size she was very seaworthy and we were able to make passages to Tenby, Stackpole Quay and Skomer Island via Jack Sound. However, the real pleasure was cruising up river to places like Lawrenny.

With a new and large mortgage on our house in Cardiff, maintenance was a DIY affair and this provided some sobering experiences. There was the time we entrusted some plywood locker lids to be chemically stripped of their varnish only to find the laminating glue was also attacked. We had a small hole in the engine exhaust pipe and we commissioned a mate in the Rotary Club (Neil joined Rotary in 1984) to bend and weld up a replacement. The bend and the diameter were all wrong, the cylinders wouldn't exhaust, the petrol wouldn't inject and petrol leaked out of the carburettor. Frightening.

As "Moonfleet" aged and needed considerable investment, we were now facing a dilemma as to which direction to go. The old advice that we should lie down in a dark room until the mood passed was probably sound but we didn't listen and lurched about. We actually bought an out and out drop keel racer on the basis it was a distress sale and going cheap. It was proudly shown to mates, sat in the drive on its trailer for a couple of weeks and then was sold on at a modest profit. We also at this stage nearly bought a Liberty 23, a David Thomas designed cat-rigged ketch which would have been ideal for the Haven. Another boat we looked at this time was the new well-designed Hunter Horizon 23.

At length, "Jacly II" was acquired. This was a well-used Southerly 28 drop keel motor sailer which met the criteria of being pretty, comfortable and practical. We were able to invite friends to stay on board without feeling cramped. My surveyor wished to inspect the swivel pin which involved me, lying under the boat in a puddle, rendering the drop keel immovable, extracting the pin, dashing to the surveyor for his approval, and then dashing back to the boat before the keel moved. The master plan worked. This was an example of why pride of ownership is a myth. Another was similar; lying in a wet puddle to apply antifouling paint (ergo liquid gold!) on a freezing February day is nobody's idea of fun, particularly when you have picked up a speeding ticket on the way. None the less we enjoyed "Jacly II" for several years both in and out of the Haven including taking part in local festivals.

Not too long after, the steel industry was in total disarray, the children had flown the nest and "Jacly" was sold away. I had to start looking elsewhere for an income stream. I set up as a consultant on my own, not much fun, but later was hired by Minton Treharne and Davis, analysts and consultants in Cardiff. I had a number of interesting assignments including climbing a Jacobs ladder in Brazil to inspect a cargo of iron ore contaminated by seawater, advising on the welding of paddles for a paddle steamer and addressing Lloyds of London on the shipment of steel cargoes. Once established with MTD, our thoughts turned to a small and easily maintained little boat. A Winkle Brig called "Brig O' Dale" became part of our life and gave us enormous pleasure for several years. We used her to trail to waters we had never visited, to visit maritime festivals and to sail, on the top of a high spring tide, to magic places like Blackpool Mill and Cresswell Quay in Pembrokeshire. Plans were laid also to take her to Pembroke and to haul her up the weir into Haverford West, but alas they never materialised. Again, more about "Brig O' Dale" later.

"Moonfleet", Skomer

"Jacly II", Dale

"Brig O' Dale", Blackpool Mill

"Brig O' Dale" at Cresswell Quay

Enterprise on the Thames

Extreme Sailing in Cardiff Bay

Heritage

An aspect of having been born in the UK is that you cannot be unaware of your maritime and colonial history. While there have been many successful dynasties and power bases over the centuries, few if any match the western seaboard nations for their aggressive colonisation of the new world of America as well as large parts of South Africa, India and South East Asia. The ambition to even contemplate these adventures is breath-taking. It was said of Cecil Rhodes that he wished to see Africa "pink" from the Mediterranean Sea to the South Atlantic. With the help of Sepoys and Mr Gatling's gun, he very nearly succeeded.

The fallout from the Industrial Revolution in the form of ships, armaments and engineering extended the opportunity. But more than this, it was the mindset that won the day; in trading you did not upset the British East Indian Company or the Hudson Bay Company. At its height as a British Colony, the hierarchy of the Indian Civil Service was populated by old boys from four English Public Schools. They were canny enough in their administration to keep the Maharajahs on board.

One of the best monuments to this larceny is the Victoria and Albert Museum in South Kensington. The building itself is an emphatic statement of wealth and competence. The treasures within come from all corners of the Commonwealth.

Sea power was the driving force of this early empire building, but there was something more natural working on behalf of the West European nations and that had to do with wind direction. The wind direction in the great oceans of the world are similar. They blow clockwise in the northern hemisphere and anticlockwise in the southern hemisphere. Hence as you leave the UK, you have a fair wind across the Atlantic. You then have the option, as the "Mayflower" and the "Matthew" did, of carrying on up the east coast of North America, or find your way through the doldrums and then ride the anticlockwise wind down the east coast of South America and across to the Cape of Good Hope. Avoiding being set on to Namibia's Skeleton Coast, a risk even today, you then round the

Cape and ride the trades up to South East Asia, India and East Africa. Similarly, your exit from the Indian Ocean was the anticlockwise winds which took you round Cape Horn. There was a perfect marriage of facility and ambition. Ships leaving the UK with cargoes of railway engines and young women looking for husbands en route to India, then cotton and opium from India to China and finally cotton and tea from China back home. Much is made of the "Cutty Sark" but she was not commercially successful. Built as a tea clipper, she was too large to pass through the newly developed Suez Canal and ended up carrying less profitable wool from Australia.

It is difficult to paraphrase the magnitude of these events, the wars fought by European Nations with vested interests, the drawing of modern geo-political maps and the enslavement of peoples. And driving it all were ships and sailors. Seen against this background, "Rule Britannia" and "Land of Hope and Glory" appear less jingoistic.

We could pay more homage. Why don't we have a Captain Cook day in memory of his many exploits, which include the discovery of Australia and New Zealand, and of the sacrifice of his life?

It is a reflection of the cult of personality that prevails in our modern world that we can produce instant heroes and heroines almost overnight. One of the most conspicuous sailors of recent times is Ellen MacArthur. Being able to broadcast live from her catamaran "B&Q" as she rounded Cape Horn was a pinnacle of both sailing and broadcasting and full reward for a young life committed to boats and sailing. But spare a thought for young Dee Caffari who one year later rounded Cape Horn to windward and barely got a mention. We came across her recently when a stage of the Volvo Ocean Race was completed in Cardiff; she was skippering an all-female crew.

Who else are the models to motivate the next generation of young sailors? Sometime before Ellen MacArthur, a mature Francis Chichester had made a conspicuous solo circumnavigation in "Gypsy Moth" and the view formed that this was a knightable exploit. In fact, Chichester was also a pilot and he was knighted for his services to navigation. He had pioneered island hopping in the South Pacific by aiming off to windward of a target landing, flying the distance (assessing distance was more accurate than assessing a course) and then turning downwind on a bearing to the target. "Gypsy Moth" later became a sail training vessel and at one stage was holed beneath the waterline.

Clare Francis' sponsored single-handed transatlantic voyage in "Robertson's Golly" attracted attention being a "her" voyage rather than a "his" voyage. Take nothing away from Clare but Nicolette Milnes-Walker had sailed across the pond from Pembrokeshire several years earlier and no one noticed. Clare Francis went on to be a famous novelist. Many of the characters in her books went to watery graves in fens and wetlands – perhaps she had demons to exorcise.

One of my favourite circumnavigators was Alec Rose ("Lively Lady") who, it was rumoured, got out of bed one morning and said to his wife, 'I'm off!'

However, for me the greatest motivator of young people to go sailing was Arthur Ransome ("Nancy Blackett") who wrote a series of books with titles like "Swallows and Amazons" and "We didn't mean to go to sea". He wrote about real children in real sailing adventures. Ransome's books can still be obtained through The Folio Society.

There have been other sailors down through the ages whose seamanship is unrivalled. The endurance and resourcefulness of Shackleton and his crew when their ship "Endurance" was trapped and crushed in the Antarctic ice is legendary. They equipped the ship's boat ("James Caird") to make an offshore passage and then sailed from Elephant Island to South Georgia (800 miles), an astonishing feat. The "James Caird" can still be seen at Dulwich College. Perversely, it was the Norwegian Amundsen who was first to the South Pole in 1911 (just ahead of Scott) in his vessel "The Fram" which had an egg-shaped hull which was lifted rather than crushed by the ice. It can be seen in one of the maritime museums in Oslo, as can the "Kon Tiki". Amundsen also explored the North East and North West passages in the Arctic and reached the North Pole albeit using a plane. He was tragically killed in an air sea rescue crash.

Other nations collectively salute mariners in different ways; outside the nautical museum on the banks of the Tagus in Lisbon is a monument dedicated to all the Portuguese navigators. Inside the museum is a wonderful collection of models made by shipbuilders for their clients. The models nod to the explosion of shipbuilding entering the twentieth century. Between 1830 and 1930, some 80% of the worlds shipping was built in the UK, much of it on the River Clyde, and assignments were remarkable. The "M.S. Yavari" was built on the Thames, taken apart, the bits shipped to South America and carried up the Andes mountains on donkeys and reassembled on Lake Titicaca, Peru. She is reminiscent of a Clyde Puffer but long waisted. Why long waisted? Steam was raised by burning llama dung and you needed a lot of it. While visiting Peru we were allowed access to the bridge; it is a great feeling to stand behind the wheel as though conning the vessel.

The twin screw steam ship "Earnslaw" is another vessel still in commission reflecting early British and Commonwealth enterprise. She was built in Dunedin, New Zealand in 1912, dismantled and transported by train to Kingston at the south end of Lake Wakatipi where she is still in use in the tourist trade. While in New Zealand we thoroughly enjoyed an excursion around the lake. She is the only coal fired commercial passenger carrying steamship in the southern hemisphere. She has port and starboard coal bunkers; when one of these is being filled, a counterweight is placed on deck above the other bunker to maintain lateral trim. We should never cease to marvel at the ingenuity of past generations.

The Matthew

B&Q

Gypsy Moth, Lively Lady, Robertson's Golly

Nancy Blackett

Lisbon, Navigators Monument

MS Yavari, Lake Titicaca, Peru

Festivals of the Sea

Our acquisition of the trailer sailer Winkle Brig ("Brig O' Dale") was a recognition that we couldn't have our cake and eat it. The family budget would have been blown apart by chartering abroad and at the same time continuing to maintain a boat like a Southerly 28. And yet the yearning for a boat of our own could not be resisted. Hence "Brig O' Dale" which was very compatible with her home port of Dale.

It was not part of the original plan but what an easily trailer-able boat opened up for us was the opportunity to attend the International Festivals of the Sea which were being run at various ports around the UK between 1996 and 2005. The Festivals were run by the co-joining of Civic and Marine Industry interests. The events we attended took place at Bristol (1996), Portsmouth (1998), Portsmouth (2001), Leith (2003) and Portsmouth (2005). We also attended the Celtic Voyage Festival at Milford Haven in 2000.

The attendees were an extraordinary fellowship of people prepared to make long voyages or to tow their boats to an event just to enjoy being surrounded by other boats and other sailors. At Leith, "Brig O' Dale" was moored at the end of a very long pontoon; returning to her even in the wee small hours took some time since a chat (lubricated) ensued at every stern.

We stayed the night with friends Kate and David Cawston, mainstays of the Brig fraternity, who were also trailering on north to our launch site which was at Granton on the Forth Estuary. We launched successfully and, with the loom of the Forth Bridge as a background, had a downwind but gloomy passage to the dock at Leith. The lock was closed to us. We found a little shelter behind a shore projection just east of Leith; we were invited to tie up to the stern of another larger yacht which is indicative of Festival spirit. We waited and waited; eventually we called the lock and were advised they were waiting for a larger vessel; fair enough, lock openings are determined by the state of the tide and the volume of traffic. The vessel turned out to be a three-masted schooner. Anyway, there was room for us all in the lock and again there was a festival atmosphere. It was dark before we were directed to our berth.

A good time was had by all. We were able to visit the Royal Yacht Britannia, Edinburgh Castle and to enjoy the presence of the Schooners Prince William, Tenacious and Oosterschelde. "Sunset" being played at the end of the evening by a Royal Marines band sent shivers up spines.

We have always subscribed to the notion of making every journey count so on our drive back from Scotland we detoured into the Lake District and relaunched on Lake Ullswater. We were rewarded with beautiful weather but with not a lot of wind for sailing. None the less, anchored in the bay on the east side of the lake, we enjoyed one of those idyllic evenings where everything is reflected in the water. The views, either from the boat to the shore or from the shore to the boat, were delightful. We had a new toy. It was a tower arrangement which sat on top of a single gas burner on which you could suspend slices of bread which toasted a treat. We also had the pleasure of a walk towards the south of the lake.

Another memorable festival was that at Portsmouth in 2001. We launched at Gosport (again mob handed with other Briggers thanks to the Cawstons) and had a short sail across to Portsmouth. This was a highly successful Festival in an ideal venue and it also built on experience derived from earlier events. It was also fun entering harbour by boat.

At the end of the Festival, we trailered round to the Beaulieu River and relaunched at a local boatyard. This was a real bonus to sail in a well renowned destination which also gave us access to the Solent and to the Medina River, Isle of Wight.

En route to the Medina, we had a sail aback. The foresail sheets consisted of a single line made fast at the clew to give equal lengths to port and starboard. The sheets were cleated off aft. For some reason we ended up with one short sheet and one long sheet; the short one was too short to allow the clew to clear forward of the mast and under load could not be released (the sail was "aback".) Hence we were pinned by a jib powering us off the wind and a main driving us up into the wind. It was a hairy moment. We put the outboard in reverse to reduce the windage while we sorted it. In sailing, constant vigilance must be the watchword. None the less, we then had an enjoyable sail in the Solent which included a night in Cowes. We took satisfaction that we had managed a difficult circumstance.

The Celtic Voyage 2000, which we again attended in the Brig, was a much quieter affair and was largely housed in the marina at Milford Haven. A much livelier occasion was the Tall Ships race in 1991 also held in Milford Haven. We were able to watch, while anchored, a sail past of a wonderful collection of vessels including those from the Sail Training Association, the Jubilee Trust and the Ocean Youth Club and also the Etoile, the Astrid, the Dar Mlodziezy and the Royal Yacht Britannia all dressed overall. We watched from the deck of our Southerly 28 with guests on board with food and wine and it was a magic experience.

The last festival we attended was at Portsmouth in 2005. Afterwards we trailed the boat down to Poole Harbour with the intention of spending a few days in these waters. However, the elements were against us and the wind and sea state were such that we were unable to launch. We waited overnight but in the morning the conditions hadn't improved so reluctantly we returned home. We had had great fun with the Brig but decided it was time to sell; the end of another era.

IFOS 2001, Portsmouth

IFOS 2005, Portsmouth

Brig on Ullswater

The Stepping Stones to Family Charters

With more time being spent on the water and ambitions building up to do more, it seemed appropriate to seek some formal seamanship qualifications, in part to have some competence reassurance but also some certification which charterers may require. In those days there was no RYA certification route; the only route available was through the Board of Trade Yachtmaster Certificate which in fact was a professional Mates Ticket without the sea-time. To obtain this you had to be proficient in Morse code and Valerie spent a long time sending signals from one side of our bedroom to the other. I duly attended an examination in Liverpool one freezing December morning. The Morse exam required you to identify each letter and to repeat it to a fellow examinee sitting next to you. I passed but I suspect my somewhat slow response to my partner was merely confirming what had already echoed around the room. The modern RYA categories provide a much better system and we are comfortable in our roles of Day Skippers.

The arrival of our two daughters Moira and Fiona inevitably constrained our nautical activities but, in many ways, it also stimulated them. How could we bring them up to follow in our footsteps? We had a cunning plan which we would commend to others.

One year we "double booked" a summer holiday, i.e. for the same week we booked our decrepit old caravan into a convenient site as a bolt hole while at the same time chartering a Westerly Pageant at a marina in the Falmouth River. The idea was if the girls were too stressed, we could retreat to the caravan. We need not have worried. The marina from where the boat was based fronted a large lagoon and, in the evening, we could put them in the dinghy attached to a long line and let them safely row off on their own. As well as it being very much to their liking, they also became quite adept at handling it.

Strangely, they also enjoyed sailing the Pageant to windward. They would lie together on the leeward bunk and, as we tacked, see how long they could stay in the bunk before it became the windward bunk and tipped them out on to the cabin sole. This event was greeted with gales of laughter.

This charter was so successful we repeated it the following year. This in turn led to similar charters, firstly, on Lake Windermere (Sabre 27). The highlight of this location was rowing the dinghy into the creek on "Wild Cat Island" amid cries of 'just like it says in the book' (i.e. Arthur Ransome's "Swallows and Amazons"). Later and again when they were still small, we took them on a Snapdragon 27 to the Kyles of Bute The "sailing" experience for young people is well grounded in the business of boat managing but always brings the unexpected, like a mink scurrying along the foredeck or having to catch the contents of your mug on the way down from where they had been projected up by a sudden movement of the boat.

Visiting this part of the world has high nostalgia for me since a boys' voyage, which figures in the Yachting Monthly article referred to earlier, was a circumnavigation of the Isle of Mull from Ardfern in a Rival 34 which of course included a visit to Tobermory. The scenic ambience was not the only memory I brought away. We had repaired to the Tobermory Hotel for a drink when we were approached by a pleasant young man who was on a photographic assignment (all expenses paid) who asked us if we would mind if he joined us. We didn't, so he did, the expense account was the tab and a good time was had by all. Our sail the next morning was a subdued affair.

This then was the background to our Chartering odyssey. Our journeys cover a period of 40 years. What follows is a chronological record of charters made, the vessels sailed and, on occasions, the other crew members who joined us. Included are descriptions of the cruising grounds, the nature of the landscapes and seascapes we have visited and the memories we returned with. Inevitably, the shorelines and the shore facilities will have changed over this length of time. However, the seasons, the elements and the vagaries of nature have not changed and we are sure that there are aspects of our descriptions which have not changed. Certainly, the details of where our seamanship went wrong are as relevant today as they ever were. It is in a sense a circumnavigation since our voyages have taken us to the fringes of all the great oceans visiting what have become the jewels of the cruising options. We feel immensely privileged that we have been afforded this opportunity.

Dressed for first charter

Rowing to "Wild Cat Island" on Lake Windermere

Lake Windermere

Enjoying the Kyles of Bute

Moira taking the helm

Bibliography (Navigation)

The following books and publications provide background and information concerning Neil and Valerie's Adventures. They are at home (well thumbed) rather than lying in some library.

Seychelles Nautical Pilot, Alain Rondeau, Praxys Marine

A Guide to Anchorages in Southwest Florida, edited by Andrew Egeressy, Boaters Action and Information League Inc.

Gulf Islands and Vancouver Island, Anne and Laurence Yeadon-Jones, Raincoast Books

Essential Sailing Destinations, foreword by Sir Robin Knox-Johnston, AA Publishing

100 Magic Miles of the Great Barrier Reef (The Whitsunday Islands), David Colfelt, Windward Publications.

Greek Waters Pilot, Rod Heikell, Imray Laurie Norie & Wilson Ltd.

Turkish Waters & Cyprus Pilot, Rod Heikell, Imray Laurie Norie & Wilson Ltd.

Ionian, Rod Heikell, Imray Laurie & Wilson Ltd.

Bay of Islands, Warren Jacobs and Nancy Pickmere, Kowhai Publishing Ltd.

The 1999-2000 Cruising Guide to the Virgin Islands, Nancy and Simon Scott, Cruising Guide Publications Inc.

Guide to Navigation and Tourism in French Polynesia, Patrick Bonnette and Emmanuel Deschamps, Editions A. Barthelemy and Editions Le Motu.

Northland Coast Boaties Atlas (The Essential Guide to New Zealands North Eastern Coast), David Thatcher, Captain Teach Press.

Vancouver, Howe Sound and the Sunshine Coast, Anne and Laurence Yeadon-Jones, Raincoast Books

Sail Thailand, John Everingham, Andy Dowden and Bill O'Leary, Artasia Press

Waterways Guide Norfolk Broads, Collins Nicholson.

Channel Harbours and Anchorages, K Adlard Coles, Nautical Publishing Company Ltd.

We would particularly recommend the Greek and Turkish Waters Pilots produced by Rod and Lucinda Heikell. These are much sailed waters and also waters with a multiplicity of intricate coast lines and islands and to co-ordinate and portray this in the way it has been done must have been a herculean task. They are a must for widespread and detailed use in these waters. The only drawback is that the massive content available means that the pilot books are hard backed and are heavy to carry around.

We would also like to draw attention to the Gulf Islands and Vancouver Island Cruising Guide produced by Anne and Laurence Yeadon-Jones. They have also produced guides to Vancouver, Howe Sound & the Sunshine Coast and to Desolation Sound & the Discovery Islands. The personal commitment required to produce these guides is exceptional and one is left with high confidence in, for example, the anchoring options suggested.

For voyage planning purposes, Google Maps are a great asset. You can focus on a destination and call up an area which can be viewed as a map or as a satellite image viewed almost horizontally (street view). At high magnification, detail is amazing showing individual boats and cars on a quay. There is also a mini google entry bar through which you can search for specific detail like data on a marin

Flotilla

Flotilla 1
Trogir, Yugoslavia, 1982

Having done a few charters in the UK with the family we decided to embark on our first charter abroad; a flotilla holiday seemed to be a good option. These were pioneering times for would be flotilla sailors to charter and for the boatyards to act as the charterers. The European scene was just getting off the ground. Chartering was being offered by emerging UK businesses but the bases were still in Yugoslavian hands; our choice, "Seven Seas", was an early entrant.

We flew in to Split and were ferried to Jelsa on the island of Hvar. In these early days one learned to be relaxed about, for example, luggage falling from the bus roof as we were transferred from Jelsa to our base at Vrboska.

Our boat was a 4 berth Maxi 84 which was to remain the vessel of choice for a small charter boat in this area for quite some time. The Maxi 84, ours was called "Trogir", was fine for a young family though forward there was merely a sleeping platform rather than a forecabin. The alternative was the larger Maxi 95.

After the usual formalities, they were more formal than today's since both parties were feeling their way, we were released on board and the charter had started. It was exciting on this the first day of our chartering odyssey with everyone milling about sorting out queries over boat's gear and the courses for the day. Many of these were resolved at a skippers meeting to which everyone, not just skippers, turned up. In later years we found crews more relaxed about only skippers attending. However, we have always believed in every adult in our crew attending; two heads are always better than one. Thus we were briefed for our first day's sail to Starigrad.

The passage took us round the scenic and much indented peninsula which projects from the north coast between Vrboska and Starigrad. With sunshine and a gentle breeze and after all our doubts, it was a perfect introduction into a flotilla in Mediterranean waters both for us and our two girls, aged 11 and 13.

Starigrad turned out to be a gem of a place with a fine quay, courtyards and narrow walkways spanned by arched buildings; a nice place to relax after our first and busy day. Typically, in recent years, on the first evening boat crews, often families, dined separately but as the days progressed there was more fellowship which culminated in group meals. This was not always the case on this flotilla since many of the overnight stops were in deserted locations. The compensation was these were often very beautiful.

The real joy of flotilla sailing in these waters kicked in the next day. We had a 20-mile passage from Starigrad to Rogac on the north coast of Solta Island passing the narrow straights at Milna. The weather was calm which allowed us time to anchor in a cove on the north coast of Solta to swim and to snorkel. These coves had a character of their own. A "cove" conjures up a beach captured by two headlands; the reality turned out to be an indented rocky shoreline with boat sized inlets so that it was a bit like having your own private dock. There was holding enough off the bow, not that you needed it, and plenty of narrow-shaped rocks which would take a bight on the end of a rope to act as a breast or stern line. Later we sailed on to Rogac to a pleasant quay in a very quiet place; today it boasts charter companies and apartments.

The next day was a change of atmosphere. From the isolation of Solta we made passage to the busy buzz of the medieval town of Trogir where we were able to moor up to the town quay. A must was to climb up the 13th century cathedral bell tower from which the views are magnificent. On a previous non-sailing visit to Trogir we had watched a performance of "Romeo and Juliet" in the main square. The girls were captivated by the silver filigree jewellery, handcrafts and immense bunches of cherries. It is a historic place full of atmosphere generated by cobbled streets and quaint historic buildings.

On departure from Trogir, we were to face a long northerly passage through open water off the west coast to Primosten; we were concerned whether this would be challenging. However, after an early departure we had time to anchor and sunbathe in another iconic cove south of Trogir and met pleasant conditions throughout. Primosten, on the mainland west coast, retained a quaintness despite quays, waterfront buildings and conspicuous navigation lights. There were stalls selling local merchandise such as pots, rugs, carpets and lace wear.

Leaving Primosten, we ran before a southerly wind further north to Sibenik with its diverting cathedral which we visited. From here we entered the inland waterway and made our way under engine to Skradin, passing under a spectacular bridge resting on tall slender pillars. Here we were able to visit the Krka falls. On a previous visit we had seen the full splendour of the falls but diversion of the water through a recently built hydro-electric station meant that the water flow down the falls had decreased somewhat. Still impressive but not so forceful and we were able to swim and play around in the pools beneath the falls.

From Skradin, we retraced our steps down the inland waterway and headed south to Zlarin Island. We had the opportunity to anchor in a cove just north of Zlarin town before moving on and securing a berth for the night in the town itself. The flotilla was rafted up bows to the quay with stern lines deployed. Conditions were perfect for a windsurf and later we were blessed with a delightful sunset.

From Zlarin it was time to retrace our steps and head back to Milna on the island of Brac. We took the opportunity to do some more windsurfing at Drvenik; the conditions here again were ideal and it was possible to carry one of the girls as a passenger on the board. Then it was on to revisiting the cove on Solta we had explored on our outward journey; this is part of the fun to carve out and identify a nice place and then, if the opportunity presents itself, to revisit it. In a sense it became "our" place and we had a nice lunch to celebrate. We spent our last night in a deserted cove on the south coast of Brac. This again provided magic windsurfing but it was difficult in a deserted cove with no beach to drum up a last night party particularly with young children involved.

We were elated by our arrival back in Vrboska. With hindsight it was all small beer but the fact remained that we had challenged ourselves by travelling with two young children to a part of Yugoslavia we had never seen before and going to sea in a boat with which we were totally unfamiliar. We all of us walked tall.

It was the start of the chartering scene for everyone involved and it had its own characteristics. The flotilla leaders were a mature couple rather than young blades and we were "mother ducked" rather than given a day's course and destination with options for stopping off and then left to get on with it. There was considerable bureaucracy with the need to register and show papers in each port. There were very few boats; most coves and destinations we had to ourselves. To obtain bread you had to shop early and it was apt to go stale by lunchtime. People were distant rather than friendly. They did have gorgeous cherries, bought by the kilo, and there were hand carved wooden artefacts. But that was then, with Yugoslavia being a communist country and before Croatia. We will see it as very different in the flotillas that follow. Flotillas for us followed inevitably from a sense of pride in what we had achieved on our first and also because we were all hooked. In the future, whenever we mentioned chartering, the girls' faces would light up.

Flotilla 2
Southern Ionian, Greece, 1983

This was our second flotilla and the first we took to the Southern Ionian. We sailed out of Sivota, Mum and Dad and the two children. Sivota lies at the head of a deep inlet situated on the south east coast of Levkas. It is a delightful place from which to sail since it has all-round protection with depths shelving to 5 metres in the centre of the bay allowing anchoring or going stern-to on the quay. Our boat was a Dufour 2800 with the local name of "Kalamos". The Dufour 2800 was widely used in the flotilla business at the time since it offered good accommodation for a family of four with high volume and a high freeboard for comfortable sailing. As well as getting our important briefing about the boat and about the area, the other priority was a visit to Yanni's Taverna.

All provisioned and on board the following morning, we were bound for Nidri. This meant navigating one of the most attractive channels in the Ionian, the Stenon Meganisiou which divides Levkas from Meganisi. Nidri lies at the northern end of the channel leading to Ormos Vlikho. Nidri allows bow or stern-to moorings to the quay but there is also scope for anchoring particularly in Tranquil Bay opposite the town with delightful trees and bushes on the hillside behind.

Flotilla life provides essentially two diversions. One is the opportunity to navigate from one overnight stop to another; the other is finding the best place to enjoy lunch and a midday swim. Places don't come much better than Abelike Bay on Meganisi Island. There are several fingers of land which project north between Port Vathi and Port Atheni. These provide scenic bays, well protected other than to the north, and with depths at their heads to facilitate anchoring. They are also ideal for water sports and we enjoyed a lunchtime stop here with windsurfing.

Our next destination was Spartakhori again on Meganisi. Spartakhori (Port Spiglia) offers anchoring at the bottom of the bay though depths allow anchoring on a large scope further out. We formed a raft stern-to to the quay. The village itself, perched high above the port, commands wonderful views and is delightful with white buildings festooned with purple bougainvillea flowers. It was well worth the climb and Laki's taverna provided welcome refreshment. Donkeys provided local transport carrying loaded panniers and the girls made a great fuss of them. Next morning, we topped up our water supply from the local well which was also the venue for skipper's briefing.

It is exciting to move on but also sad that you can't spend longer in a nice place. But move on we must, with Kioni our next stop. We paused to explore the cave of Papa Nicolis and in the calm conditions Valerie and the girls rowed the dinghy right inside while skipper Neil waited circling just outside.

The joy of being in these waters was enhanced by our arrival at Kioni. Kioni was a delightful place to be; it was fronted by a narrow quay with white houses behind with a wooded slope climbing behind. We rafted off to bow lines and pulled dinghies to the beach by means of the stern lines. We were part of the village and marvelled (or rather were horrified) at the sight of octopuses being beaten ahead of cooking.

Fiskardo beckoned and we enjoyed the best of both worlds. We enjoyed a calm lunch on route but later had a brisk beat to test our seamanship. Fiskardo and Kioni have the same ambience; both delightful little ports. In Fiskardo we were able to be stern-to with our cockpits part of the village. Shops selling local handcrafts were also close by.

The next objective was Aghia Eufimia via the Stenon Ithakis channel. En route we anchored in Agriossiki Bay just NE of Aghia Eufimia. We christened this bay "White Pebble Beach" and swam in beautiful clear turquoise waters. We moored bows to the quay in yet another delightful port. Much of it was destroyed in the 1953 earthquake and although it stayed neglected for a number of years it was now becoming a busy port again. We went by taxi to the Mellisani Cave with its stalagmites and enjoyed being taken around by the boatman.

Vathi on the Island of Ithaca was our next stopover. It is a large harbour and conditions were ideal in the evening for board sailing. We revisited Kioni before moving on to Nisis Atoko. We anchored in "One House Bay" with its high cliffs and a fine beach. It is an island which was once inhabited but now its only resident is a lone donkey. We went ashore and checked the well to ensure he had access to water; alas he was not to be found.

Never count your chickens. We had enjoyed perfect weather but there was sting in the tail; on our arrival at Pandelimon Bay on the mainland we encountered stormy weather. However, the next morning dawned fine and the spacious estuary provided a good area for yet more windsurfing.

Our free sailing took us to the Dhragoneras Islands, then on to Kastos and Kalamos, to "little" Vathi on Meganisi and finally Abelike Bay. Abelike Bay was the venue for the "rubber duck" dinghy race and the flotilla traditional BBQ. Instructed by the lead crew to collect firewood, we found a fallen tree which we dragged into service much to the amusement of the other crews.

The final day's activity, another flotilla tradition, was the yacht race back to base at Sivota. Flotillas work. They work even better with a good Flotilla Provider, in this case "Island Sailing", and with good company who often go on to be good friends. Hi to Victor, Muriel, Steff and Pete.

First Ionian Flotilla

"Rubber duck" Racing

Flotilla 3
Sporades, Greece, 1984

We were able to enjoy this "Island Sailing" flotilla in what for us was a new area and also since we again had the pleasure of the family, Moira aged 15 and Fiona 13, who were with us. Apart from the Halkidiki area, this is the most northerly cruising area on the east coast of Greece. It has numerous islands to visit. Our boat was called "Altair" – the type of boat she was is alas lost in the annals of time.

We flew into Skiathos; the approach to the runway is directly over Skiathos bay so while on the plane landing or on the ground watching planes taking off these were diverting experiences. We were taken to our base and able to complete the formalities ready to get under way the following morning. Our first passage was from Skiathos to Koukounaries Bay on the south side of the Island. This was a delightful bay with a beautiful sandy beach backed by a fringe of palm trees.

Our next destination was Panormou Bay on the south side of Skopelos Isalnd. En route we enjoyed a lunch time stop at an idyllic bay on Tsoungria Island. Panormou Bay wrapped itself around you as you entered and gave a sense of seclusion. We enjoyed a beautiful sunset and were fortunate not to experience a katabatic wind which sometimes can roll down from the mountains into the inlet. We rowed ashore to a taverna in the evening and our oars displayed phosphorescence.

Our next port of call was Skopelos Town. We made a lunch time stop at Stafilos Bay on the south west corner of Skopelos Island where conditions were ideal for windsurfing. Skopelos, the main town on Skopelos Island, boasts a fine defensive quay which gives shelter to a large area to receive ferries and visiting yachts. It was a delightful place with quaint streets, white buildings and a prominent church. They were catching up as a resort. Our pursuit of a shower was rewarded by our being passed through several parties to a private house with a large bathroom. Who says private enterprise is dead?

Our intended target the next day was Steni Vala, mid-way up the east coast of Alonnisos Island. En route we anchored off Votsi, a smallish bay well protected by headlands, where we swam and windsurfed. Still pursuing our northerly course, we took lunch in Tzortzi which is protected behind the red rock headland of Kokkinokastro. We pressed on to Steni Vala. Steni Vala is a busy port with considerable fishing and other commercial craft. The flotilla leader was not comfortable with the space available to us so reluctantly we returned to Votsi.

Votsi does not have a large capacity but we found space to anchor. After our protracted previous day and the fact that Votsi was a pleasant place, we were in no mood to leap up early and be off. It also became apparent that the weather was going to be stormy not only through the day but continuing into the next day. Since we were secure where we were and unwilling to risk a combination of bad weather and full moorings and anchorages, we stayed put for three nights.

The following morning, at long last we made our passage to Steni Vala. It was a lively beat with unpredictable heeling. Valerie, who likes to travel standing on the cabin to cockpit steps with her shoulders poking through the hatch ended up on the cabin sole. However, this was the only privation and we made it to Steni Vala, a sheltered bay and on this occasion with space to anchor.

We had a free sailing the next day. We chose with three other boats to visit Port Vasiliko on the west coast of Peristeri Island. The island lies off the east coast of Alonnisos with the same SW to NE alignment. Peristeri was un-inhabited at the time of our visit and it made for a very relaxing overnight stay with good windsurfing options.

The next day presented difficulties. There was a cable running on the floor of the bay (one is marked on modern charts) and, as we weighed anchor, our flukes caught under the chain. 0/10 for not buoying the anchor, 10/10 for tracing the cable to the shore line, passing a bight of rope under it and tugging the bight to the stern of the boat. Lifting the bight of rope vertically freed the flukes and we were under way free sailing to Steni Vala.

Steni Vala is a sheltered rectangular bay some 200 metres in length, shallow and surrounded by gentle tree clad hills. With limited depth, we had bow anchors and stern lines to the shore. The place was a sheer delight; it is no surprise that the bay has been developed over the years (see our visit in the Sporades in 2016). We were saddened by the news that one of the boats we had been with in Port Vasiliko had also met anchor problems and a lady had damaged her hand.

We reluctantly had to move on and had two days to fill ahead of our arriving in Patitiri. We were spoiled for choice as to where to hold the Flotilla Barbecue. Morning after recollections were that this was at Tzortzi with its reddish rock foreshore and isolated buildings nestling in the trees on the north shore. There was no time for hangovers for passage was needed to the port of Patitiri to the south. We were fortunate not to meet any ferries as we entered the harbour. It is a very attractive place with cliffs to the south and pine clad hills above. The thing to do at Patitiri is to take a taxi up to the ruined village of Alonnisis on the hill above. It was in the process of being restored and the views from up there are spectacular.

We were nearing the end of two wonderful weeks and, after a lunch time stop at Agnondas on Skopelos Island, we were bound back to Panormou Bay. We had good weather in Agnondas with wind from the south and the surfboard out. It is not so ideal in a southerly when a swell rolls in. From here we had a passage round Cape Mirti up to the bay at Panormou. We tacked into Panormou before lying to stern anchors with a bow line ashore. It was wonderful to windsurf against a backcloth of a rocky shore adjacent to trees with reddish rock outcrops.

Our next port of call was to revisit Koukounaries. We had hoped to have more time to enjoy its obvious charm. However, this was not to be since we had a severe weather warning (summer winds tend to be northerly and Koukounaries is low lying to the north). The whole flotilla was directed to a refuge in a small creek which lies in the north east corner of the bay. We were two abreast and bow to stern all the way up the creek. Strangely, the night was quiet.

On the morrow, we were relaxed. The hard work was over and we were in the mood to party before our return to Skiathos. The party commenced with a dinghy race; the most conspicuous skill on display was foul play. Later the yachts took place in a race back to base; we were second. (We make a habit of this; we should have won a race round Kalamos Island on flotilla in the Southern Ionian in 2011, q.v.). So it was all over and hailed as a success by all. Our departure from Skiathos the following morning went smoothly.

Koukounaries Bay

Flotilla 4
Southern Ionian, Greece, 1985

This flotilla was a milestone in as much that it represented our fourth flotilla and also a return to the Ionian, the place that provided us with the incentive and motivation to undertake flotilla and bareboat charters over the years. It also offered us a return to one of the most attractive destinations. The other exceptional outcome was that it provided three families with young children the opportunity of a lifetime of shared fellowship. The core attitudes were such that we went on to sail together, to ski together, to cycle together and to see our issues mature into their careers and to find their life partners. In short, we were blessed. Sadly, we lost touch with two other couples one of whom went sail about educating kids along the way and the other dealing with vicissitudes of the oil industry.

The flotilla started at Sivota which sits at the southern end of the island of Levkas which was memorable in its own right but enhanced by the presence of Yanni's Taverna.

Our first port of call was Nidri on the island of Levkas. Nidri lies on a narrow neck of sea which allows access to the land locked bay of Ormos Vlikho – it seems extraordinary that in recent years a storm raced through the bay throwing yachts up on to the shore. Nidri was busy and there was a certain amount of chaos in getting the boats rafted out.

From Nidri we moved on to Port Atheni on Meganisi Island. Port Atheni is the most easterly of the finger bays which lie on the north-east corner of Meganisi. The sheltered nature of the bay makes it ideal for windsurfing. Our next destination was Spartakhori (alias Port Spiglia) again a spacious sheltered bay sitting at the middle of the Meganisi north shore. The place was made to relax in and the relaxation took a number of forms. The first was on the hilltop at Laki's Taverna where it was decreed that the kids would dine at a separate table from the adults (I'm not sure who was knighted for this suggestion). We were also provided with the opportunity to join in Greek dancing. In the midst of this heaven on earth were the pretty streets and bougainvillea flowers.

We would have lingered but we were moved on this time to Fiskardo which lies at the head of the Stenon Ithakis channel between Ithaca and Cephalonia. It was a delightful place with white houses standing adjacent to the quay. At our lunchtime stop between Fiskardo and Osmos Polis the preoccupation was how many children can stand on a windsurfer (sans sail) and maintain stability.

Ormos Polis, a generous bay but somewhat exposed to the south, makes a nice stop with a wooded shoreline rising steeply behind rock fringed water. On the left coast of the bay is the cave of Loizos, believed to be a temple of worship to Odysseus. A walk up the hill to Stavros takes you to a museum in which are displayed objects found as a result of excavations in the cave. A sculpted bust of Odysseus is prominent in the main square of the village. The youngsters were ahead of us and we met them coming back down declaring that all there was to see were 'a lot of broken pots'!

From Ormos Polis a course was laid for Ayias Eufimia which lies on the east side coast of Cephalonia opposite the south end of Ithaca. Here we had a most unusual encounter with Tim Severin following the course of the original voyage of Odysseus in his replica galley "Argo". At his request, the flotilla set sail surrounding the "Argo". Cameras rattled at the prospect and a crew member from the "Argo" actually boarded our boat and climbed the mast to take pictures of the occasion. These pictures appear in the book "The Ulysses Voyage" and featured in an article in the National Geographic Magazine.

It was time to head to the town of Vathi on Ithaca where dusk presented us with a beautiful sunset. We also had the presence of a two-masted schooner which was elegance personified. Then on to Kioni which was easily discerned on approach by three windmills on the southerly promontory. Here the weather was persistently balmy and the adults slept in the cockpit. An eccentricity was a beachside loo behind a green door which required that you took your flush bucket with you.

Our next destination was Kastos and we had the opportunity for our lunchtime stop to revisit Atoko Island, nicknamed "Donkey Island" on our previous visit. Kastos Island, which we did not know at the time, would come to haunt us. On a later flotilla we had been leading in the race in the smallest boat but when rounding the end of Kastos en route to Kalamos town, we went looking for wind instead of steering the shortest course and ended up second.

The following night was to be spent at Port Astakos on the mainland at the head of a deep bay and boy was it hot (40C.) As we sailed up the channel it felt like a hair drier blowing down from the mountain; fortunately, it did not give us any katabatic wind. We had a frantic search for ice but everywhere was closed. However, come the evening the town was alive with promenaders.

Still there was mileage and distraction to pursue which was provided by a period of free sailing. Next up were the Dhragonera Islands which gave us lunchtime snorkelling before moving on to Port Leone on Kalamos Island. The village of Port Leone is now deserted (they lost their water supply in the 1953 earthquake). There is no transport available on the island and, for example, building materials are moved around by donkey. During free sailing we linked up with four other families to form the "alternative flotilla" and enjoyed a beach BBQ together.

Returning heralds the flotilla end and return we must, this time to Meganisi and Port Spiglia. Here we dined at Taverna Spiglia and selected the best wine from the cellar. Proximity of a well provided the opportunity to wash hair in fresh water! It is interesting to reflect on how facilities have changed; in those early flotilla days there was no hot water and no showers on board. The alternative was to fill a garden spray container or a black plastic bag and strap it to the mast during the day to warm up in the sunshine.

Finally, the joy of Abelike Bay for our last evening with the traditional beach BBQ and dinghy race. In the morning and before we commenced our journey home, we were chastened by the sight of a flock of sheep "clearing" up the debris we had left behind the night before.

The conclusion of the flotilla was the yacht race back to base and the last group supper at Yanni's taverna.

It is worth taking a little time over this flotilla to break it down so that it will live on with us. We enjoyed and carried away with us as a basis of experience and future expectation:

- quiet secluded bays with little yacht congestion
- in a small boat, we could anchor close to shore
- itinerary of short distances enables lunch time activities
- quiet mornings with good sailing conditions in the afternoon
- experience of a variety of mooring techniques

- beer cooled by towing it behind in a string bag
- ideal for teenagers mixing together on a range of fronts
- the establishment of life-long friends

"Argo" surrounded by flotilla. Tim Severin's "Ulysses Voyage"

Kids having fun

Donkey transporting building materials

Hair washing using water from the well

Flotilla 5
Dubrovnik, Yugoslavia, 1987

After three years of exploring the Greek Islands, we returned to Yugoslavia with "Island Sailing". Our eldest daughter Moira was about to set off to University to read medicine and we had a feeling that this might be our last family holiday together.

Yugoslavia was still a communist country but not with quite the extreme regulation we had experienced on our previous visit. However, we did find that most restaurants offered the same "state" menu and people were rather dour. We commenced the flotilla from Dubrovnik's Marina on the River Ombla 6km from the City. The source of the river is the emergence of an underground stream which flows out of the base of cliffs and down past the marina.

After the usual bustle of settling into our boats and receiving briefing on both the boats and the flotilla procedures, we were off the following morning down the river en route to Sipanska Luka on the island of Sipan. The town is located on the northwest of the island, at the head of a deep fiord-like inlet penetrating almost half way down the island. On our way we were spoiled for choice as to which secluded bay we used to stop for lunch and a swim. Meeting up with clear turquoise water is always a great delight.

From Sipanska Luka, we made passage to Okuklje on the north east coast of the island of Mijet. A feature here was an early morning walk along a forest trail with a fantastic view overlooking the bay. The charm of these waters is that you don't have to move on to get a sense of moving on; every bay has its own story to tell. This was exemplified by the fact we spend a further night alongside at Pomena at the northwest end of Mijet. The ambience for dining, at the water's edge, was very attractive and made more so by features where wine was dispensed by tap from barrels located in niches in the stonework. Finally add in a fish restaurant serving mussels and fresh lobsters to die for and a really great time was had by all.

The well-known names on the coast raised expectations as we approached Korcula Island. We were rafted up but while ashore gusting winds caused the raft to spin resulting in lines crossed and a lot of unravelling for the lead crew. No matter since Korcula town combined both being buzzy while at the same time attractive. The route to the upper town via impressive steps passed colourful market stalls and led through narrow streets and squares.

There was now momentum in the flotilla as we moved on to an anchorage at Trstenik, a bay on the south side of the Peljesac peninsula, a mainland peninsular running northwest from Ston. As part of our stay here flotilla guests were taken by two boats round to a sheltered beach for a BBQ. It was a short passage the following day to Ston which you approach by rounding Otok Olipa at the south of the projection before turning north to Ston.

Ston was a mixture of the real and the surreal. The real was that oysters were the dish of the day. The surreal was the smell from the saltpans, which led to Ston being nicknamed by the younger members of the flotilla "Stinky Ston", and the procedure for water collection. This involved suspending a water carrier on an oar which was then shouldered by two people, filling it from the fountain in the town square and returning to the boat. If you were not tired after this, you were by the time you had walked round the impressive defensive stone walls built in the 14th century.

Lopud beckoned (local place names do not sound romantic) but this proved to be attractive. The island of Lopud lies to the southeast of Sipan Island and the main town is also called Lopud. This is a busy holiday town with a promenade lined with cafes and market stalls. Local woven carpets are a popular item.

We were entering the tail end of our flotilla time but still found diversion. We were headed next for the mainland town of Cavtat, south of Dubrovnik. This proved to be a lively seaside resort and conveniently we could lie to the quay. There was an attractive place to dine where there was also a dance floor. Replete and well oiled, the adults rose and began to prance about on the floor (prance is a more accurate description of what took place than dance). The kids fled to escape the embarrassment; the pied piper would have been impressed at their pace. Before departure the following day, we had a pleasant walk round the wooded southern peninsula.

And so all good things must end and we made passage back to the Komolac Marina. We stopped to have a final windsurf on the basis if you don't use a skill you will lose it. As we found in 2008 when we again visited this area, the Base takes the view that the best way to see Dubrovnik is to take a bus tour from the Marina. Dubrovnik has been an important citadel over many centuries and the walls and a protected harbour speak to this. However, its modern role as a tourist centre is evident with streets polished by pedestrians, throngs of visitors walking the walls and everywhere queues for a seat or a coffee. Nevertheless, it was a privilege for us to be in a timeless place. Indeed it is worth stretching the accolade to include the whole cruising ground that we had covered.

Water carrying at Ston

Carpet Stall at Lopud

Moira windsurfing

Flotilla 6
Trogir, Yugoslavia, 1988

Although we had expected the previous year's flotilla would be the last for the family, 1988 saw us back in Yugoslavia. This time we returned to the area of our first flotilla which was with Seven Seas in 1982. We joined a flotilla with Island Sailing again and were able to sail in a Maxi 84 named "Iz".

What a difference the six years had made; now the yacht chartering scene had expanded and marinas had been developed. Our base was in one of these new marinas at Primosten, no longer a quaint town with a small harbour. The good news was that despite the arrival of marinas, beautiful anchorages with clear turquoise water were still in abundance.

We had a peaceful and delightful start to the flotilla by anchoring for our first night in a deep bay south of the Razanj peninsula. The bay narrows down almost to the proportions of a river but with scope and depth to allow an anchor at the bow and a stern line ashore. The shoreline presents as white fringed rocks at the water's edge with trees on the ground rising from the edge; very typical of these waters. It was the perfect start to a flotilla with a full programme ahead of us.

Our sights were set on revisiting Trogir but we had the opportunity first to visit a bay on the south coast of Drvenik Island en route. We had fine weather and a between a tack and a reach course in a pleasant breeze. The bay was quite spacious but a U-shaped projection from the middle of the shore made for two secluded and protected areas either side, ideal for wind surfing. We were able to relax and enjoy a peaceful evening before facing the morrow with an early start to visit Trogir.

We arrived in Trogir about mid-day and were directed to the marina where we berthed; we could no longer berth against the town quay. Trogir itself seemed unchanged since we were last here and still possessed its medieval charm. It is a well-known historic town attracting many visitors. We climbed the bell tower to admire the clock tower in the main square and the views across the town. Alas, the arrival of our visit was injudicious since while we were at the top, the bell began to ring nearly deafening us. The climb itself was quite un-nerving as the steps at the last stage clung to the outer walls and had no handrail. For all this, it was still a great place to relax and enjoy the cafes and the stalls with souvenirs. We stayed for a second night.

Trogir is one of those places you leave reluctantly but press on we must. Our destination on this leg was to a bay on the north of Solta Island from where we could move on to Milna en route to Hvar. The bay we chose was wide and spacious as well as allowing us to raft up with bow anchors ashore with stern anchors laid. Once again, the vista of gentle tree lined slopes falling to a white rocky shoreline induced the flotilla maxim of 'it doesn't get much better than this'. It was also a place made for boardsailing. On approach, there is also a narrow bay flanked by a rocky shore to port with a tree covered rocky slope climbing from the shore.

We left Solta Island and made our way to Milna on the western end of the island of Brac. The sheltered bay has a prosperous past with many elegant buildings and a long waterfront which can readily accommodate a flotilla. It was a pleasant and interesting place to stay. A conspicuous landmark in Milna is the church tower in the traditional style which dominates the landscape. Another attractive feature was the town quay which is in the form of a rectangle open at one end but giving access to the other three. This leaves plenty of scope for stern-to mooring with easy access to local shops and tavernas. We were able to make use of both ambiences. Milna is a harbour which is also a traffic junction; it sees traffic going east-west between Solta and Brac and also going north-south between the Split area and Hvar Island. This was indicated by the passing of fast-moving ferries. However, prolonging our stay was not an option and we were up early on the following day to make passage to the bays on the northwest corner of Hvar. Here we were conveniently situated for a visit to Hvar harbour the following day. It was a gentle sail with young somnolent bodies decorating the deck.

An early start was embraced to ensure as much time in Hvar as possible. Fortunately, we arrived early enough to find a spot to anchor in the harbour and dinghy ashore. Then it was post-haste to explore the town. Ashore was a treasure trove of old tower-abutted buildings, a vibrant quay and a steep but shady cactus lined walk leading to the citadel. Here there were views over the roofs below of the harbour entrance. A film script could not have presented it any better. Alas time was short and we had a passage to make to the security of the Palmitzana Marina on the north coast of St Klement Island which lies just south west of the west end of Hvar. Short as our visit had been, we were very pleased that we had managed our day to include an anchored stop, a worthwhile visit and a comfortable marina at the end of it.

But hey, flotillas are about passages and fun on the way and next day we got back in the groove in a bay on the south side of Brac Island for our evening BBQ. We were all lined up tidy with stern lines secure and bow lines on the shore. Surviving photographs show late night revels with exotic eating (whole melon slices by hand), bottle laden tables and cocktail competitions. The latter was becoming a tradition on flotilla holidays; each crew mixed a cocktail which they presented in poetic terms for the lead crew to judge. The passage to Rogac the following day was a sombre affair. Rogac town and quays lie in an inlet to the west of a large bay open to the north and are well sheltered. There are three other much smaller bays which offer only partial shelter from the north. The Flotilla disgraced itself by staging a dinghy race with no rules; i.e. turning someone else's dinghy upside down as you pass was a legitimate tactic to win the race.

The following day on passage to Drvenik we had a serious race between the yachts which was to normal racing rules; I am pleased to report we were third. This was much appreciated by our daughters who had joined in the debate about sheet settings and courses steered. This put icing on the cake and the feeling of satisfaction prevailed into our last anchorage taken in the Drvenik area. It remained for us then to make passage back to Primosten which we did via Rogoznica where we took lunch. While anchored here we watched a large floating crane making passage to the north which is not a sight you meet every day. When we arrived at Primosten later in the day, the reason for the crane's voyage became apparent. A very elegant wooden sailing vessel had sunk at her moorings; the only parts of the vessel still above the waterline were her masts together with the wheel and timber guard rails mounted right aft. A sad sight indeed but also a reminder that at sea, in any circumstances, vigilance is everything. At Primosten, we also had a final flotilla meal during which we received a suitably printed plate as a race prize which was very nice. Flotilla sailing in well maintained boats in attractive sailing areas is always satisfying. We flew out of Primosten the following morning with a strong sense that we would be back, if not here but somewhere else to derive pleasure from company, seamanship, passages, town quays and picturesque bays. Little did we know at that stage how often we would be back.

Sunken yacht

Flotilla 7
Knidos, Turkey, 1997

On this flotilla we were joined by Geoff and Pat, two very close friends from Cardiff with whom we have many interests including sharing sailing activity off the Pembrokeshire Coast. However, this was to be sharing of a different type, joining a flotilla with an extensive itinerary off the south coast of Turkey and very much in the area of the Turkish holiday scene. It proved socially and nautically a great success.

We commenced our flotilla at English Harbour, a well sheltered retreat located in Degirmen Bay which sits on the south east corner of the Gulf of Gokova. The name English Harbour derives from its use as a Special Boat Squadron base in the Second World War. The nature and location of the base was such that the business of getting us to sea was readily achieved. Once on our way in an Oceanis 352 called "Lavanta" in good but hazy weather, we made passage to the rocky island of Sehir Adalasi where we took lunch. Then it was on to Akbuk Limani where in good flotilla tradition we had a punch party followed by a group meal at the Altas Taverna. Akbuk Limani lies on the south of the mainland tucked behind the peninsula of Karaburun.

The pattern settled very quickly; part of the passage in the morning before a lunch stop and then on to the day's destination in the evening. So the next day we motor sailed to Tuzla on the south side of the Gulf of Gokova and were rewarded only, alas, with a cold swim. This left us with another 9-mile-long close-hauled motor sail back past the power station to the opposite side of the Gulf and on to the small port of Cokertme. Here we had a group supper at Captain Ibrahim's restaurant with the host presiding and smoking his hookah pipe. Years later we found ourselves again in Captain Ibrahim's restaurant and happened to mention our earlier visit. The fatted calf was immediately slain and Captain Ibrahim raised from his sick bed to welcome old guests. It was very touching.

Still heading west, the morrow was again a challenging close-hauled passage at 6 to 7 knots against a strong westerly and finally having a determined tack up the Karada Channel into Bodrum. Anchoring/mooring in Bodrum was very difficult due to cross winds, narrow channels and the need for short stern lines. We relaxed after a hard day with dinner at the Mausoleum Café where the waiter had a struggle with removing the cork from a wine bottle and after the third attempt exclaimed with some unprintable words! We moved on to coffee in the Marina Club. Unusually for these waters, the wind maintained its strength throughout the night. We spent the following morning in Bodrum visiting the Castle, sampling beers on the waterfront and having lunch at the Marina, all the while marvelling at the variety of craft in the harbour from a four-masted cruise ship ("Wind Spirit"), parascending outfits and even "a stop me and buy one" ice cream merchant. Come the afternoon it was time to move on, this time to a beautiful anchorage we christened the "Blue Lagoon"; this we reached sailing some 3 miles south west at a speed of 4kts.

This was a gem of a place being essentially an oblong shaped bay wide open at one end and surrounded by a rocky white shoreline with the ground rising behind it to tree lined slopes. The white shoreline emphasises the blueness of the water and hence the title "Blue Lagoon". We stayed overnight and marvelled at its beauty; none the less in a bay being open at the top and wide open at the bottom the water temperature was quite cool.

From the Blue Lagoon we were heading for Knidos. We needed the engine at the start but later found a fresh breeze which gave us the opportunity to tack towards the south. Knidos lies at the western end of the Datca Peninsula and on approach the lighthouse on the top of Cape Krio is conspicuous. Again the wind was light and westerly and we motor sailed to make good the distance arriving at Knidos in the middle of the day. We were welcomed by Captain Ockar, harbourmaster and restauranteur.

One of the "must do's" in Knidos later in the day is to visit the ancient amphitheatre. Again, Neil embarrassed everyone by rendering his "to be or not to be" party piece; in a place like this not doing it seems a wasted opportunity. Later we took a swim in Knidos Bay; the bay is deep and as you dive the water is cool; it quickly warms as you come up to the surface. We dined ashore on barbecued barracuda with salad which was expensive but beautifully presented and served.

We woke the next morning to N.W. gusts funnelling across the northern isthmus. We had a great downwind sail heading east and logging 9 knots. We rounded Ince Burnu and met very rough conditions in Datca Bay. We eventually took in the genny and sailed under main only. However, this was insufficient for the conditions and we were suddenly over-canvassed and we did a spectacular broach. Valerie who had been standing in the hatchway was pitched down into the cabin. This was a classic instance of failing to react to changing conditions (See Pearls from Our Mudbanks). We eventually anchored off shore at Kuruca Buku and dinghyed ashore for provisions and showers. Later a taxi boat took us ashore for a meal at a campsite from where we were conducted by a torch wielding cyclist to a restaurant in the trees. We had a good meal but too much meze. We were ferried back to our boat and had a relatively quiet night.

The morrow brought fickle winds and having put the sails up and down twice we opted to motor. Selimiye, our destination, has only recently had facilities for receiving a number of yachts so we had to wait patiently to be called in to moor up. Once in it proved to be a pleasant place and a short walk took us to a cove which gave us a relaxing swim. Chocolate, fudge cake and ice cream followed at Annie's Café. The final indulgence of this very relaxed day was sea bream at the Falcon Restaurant. A restless night followed either due to overindulgence or waves lapping against the hull.

We spent the following morning in Selimiye (Port Losta) climbing up behind the village to look at a 1000-year-old tree, a tower house and the spectacular views. We had a problem freeing our anchor but once resolved we were under way towards Orhaniye. Our mid-day stop was in an unusual bay formed by volcanic rocks which appeared like giant termite nests. We had a great sail up to Orhaniye achieving 9.2 knots. There was a Sunsail Jetty waiting for us. Again of an evening we were feted, this time with a huge meze, fruit presented with sparklers and complementary Crème-de-Menthe.

The morning saw an early start towards Dirsek (Sock Bay), first to fuel up at the marina and then tacking in very light winds: we were becalmed for an hour. We were entertained by a helicopter landing at a posh hotel with a funicular train to the beach. Stooged around looking for a suitable lunch stop and ended up at the east end of Koca Isle which we christened "Cormorant Bay". After a swim and lunch, we had a frustrating sail in very light winds but reaching Dirsek eventually and rafting up. This was a nice enclosed place to be with turquoise water. After a windsurf by Neil, it was back to self-indulgence in the form of a beach BBQ which featured chicken, jacket potatoes, garlic bread, raki and beer. Party games included a mug walk, pot tug of war and fender running all of which were hilarious. The singing was a bit second rate.

The next day, we started off with a short walk up the hill for a photo session meeting "hundreds" of goats on the path. Once under way, towards our destination of Ova Buku, we had two hours of glassy calm while we progressed under engine. At length and after rounding Ince Point, we had a beat up the coast. This was slow progress due to backwinding from cliffs. At Ova Buku we were able to moor alongside the jetty, then shopped in light rain in a very "mini" market. Another group meal followed at "Ogur's Place" which offered us good food (chicken), good service and good value.

On the morrow we got back to serious sailing with breakfast taken at sea as we rounded Knidos point at 9 am en route to Amazon Creek. With very little wind, we were under engine until 11 am and thereafter motor sailing arriving at our Amazon Creek destination early afternoon. After a swim from the boat to a bathing platform and back, we took the dinghy ashore to walk through the pine trees to a campsite where beer was on offer. We walked back to the beach through a doorframe complete with door but with no fences either side of the frame! There were tortoises, rabbits and chickens and a notice which read: "Don't feed the crocodiles!" What we saw was what we saw and not a consequence of the beer! In the evening, Pat and Geoff kindly prepared an anniversary supper to celebrate Valerie and Neil's 31st Wedding Anniversary.

The following day we were due at Kargili Koyu (Kargili Village) but first an early morning walk to the campsite for provisions. We set sail into a strong breeze funnelling in from the west, initially close hauled but later more of a broad reach as we headed north. We broke our journey at Yedi Adalari entering by the south entrance. This is not a hospitable place in a strong westerly wind as the swell can penetrate through the several entrances to the anchorages. We therefore made a decision to motor on departing through the northern exit. This was quite tricky as rocks were obscured by the choppy sea (described by a fellow Yorkshire crew as 'a bit lumpy'!) and Valerie stood as lookout on the bow. Kargili Koyu is a deep sock of a bay on the south coast of the Gokova Gulf offering both shelter and a wooded ambience ashore.

Time was running out on us and return to English Harbour was the next focus. However, before leaving Kargili we took the dinghy ashore to visit Ali Baba's pond which was alive with very noisy croaking frogs. Then after a brief lunch sadly we had to make for the "Harbour" which we shared with a Mr Big and a Mr

Enormous. Our last day was eventful comprising a race followed by supper and prize giving. In the race we were one of two smaller boats taking part and became becalmed at the furthest part of the course and hence picked up the wooden spoon. We also had to pay a raki forfeit for causing the lead crew anchoring hassle along the way. The flotilla hostess ("Cloggy") was serenaded with, 'If you knew Cloggy like we know Cloggy!' In other simple words, a good time was had by all which is emblematic of flotilla life.

The following morning, we left the Sunsail Base at 9.45 am. After a stop at a roadside café with a water garden complete with turtles, we crossed the border from romance to reality as the airport signs appeared at the roadside.

Knidos Lighthouse

Windy sail before the broach!

Flotilla 8
British Virgin Islands, 2000

Getting a two boat 8 persons charter off the ground poses more than the usual issues. None the less we secured two weeks in 40' CC Beneteau Oceanis yachts, "Dodger" and "Silver Eagle", for 2 crews of 4. Seven of us flew in to St Thomas on the American Virgin Islands and transferred by ferry to the Sunsail base at Maya on Tortola. The 8th member flew in to Tortola later that day. The friends who joined us were those we first met on the Ionian flotilla in 1985. Janet and David Dick joined us on "Dodger" and Kay and Bill Abbott with their friends Maggie and Nigel took charge of "Silver Eagle".

Day one was a settling in day practising man overboard 3 times with cushions and getting used to dinghy trips to shore. Then we set sail to the Bight on Norman Island. There we were introduced to the practice of using mooring buoys, for which fees are collected, instead of anchoring. We repaired to Billy Bones's for a Group supper and to meet our companions. "Silver Eagle" was delayed by a steering fault and joined us the next morning.

Despite the promise of sea and sun, we were confronted the following morning with 3 hours of tacking down to the west coast of Salt Island. We had hoped to snorkel over the wreck of the "Rhone" but were met by a considerable swell; the snorkelling was abandoned. We moved on to find sheltered moorings on Cooper Island enabling us to gather ashore in the evening for a group cocktail party. Such events greatly enhance the sense of belonging which we have invariably met while flotilla sailing.

Next day we were favoured by a good beam reach sail north east to the small island of Marina Cay; it lies to the south of Great Camanoe and Scrub Island. The best approach is to circle the Cay to the east and approach the moorings from the north. The Cay provides a walk through flowers to the top of the island. There was food and drink to be had on the beach; strong currents off the beach were not conducive to snorkelling. A flotilla happy hour party on the beach was followed by a BBQ on the boat which required regular re-ignition (three boxes of matches!). This wasn't the Med where the winds die overnight.

We now had to make passage to Spanish Town on Virgin Gorda Island, a busy place with an excellent marina and the opportunity to shop for necessities and provisions. We took a taxi down to The Baths, a shoreline with a most unusual formation of large granite boulders which have been worn smooth by the tide. A trail ran through rocks and caves to a beautiful beach. Then it was back to The Rock Café in Spanish Town for a meal. (The Rock Café is still in business today).

The following day commenced with a long reach which would take us half way towards Anegada. We broke up the day with a lunch time stop at Drakes Anchorage off Mosquito Island before moving on to Biras Creek where we had an evening meal in the Fat Virgin Café. After our meal we moved on to the delightful Biras Creek Hotel where we enjoyed celebratory cocktails and spectacular views.

We were now set for Anegada. Anegada is very different to the rest of the BVI being comprised of low-lying coral and limestone rather than having derived from volcanic peaks. We overtook the lead boat and led the fleet all the way registering 10 to 11 knots. There are numerous reefs and we were fortunate to have clear overhead sunlight as we approached Pomato and Setting Points and the green buoy between them which marks the anchoring and moorings options. The place has an ethereal appeal. We went ashore and took a taxi ride to Loblolly Bay where strong currents offshore were apparent through the rain. We settled for beach-combing as a diversion. Once back at the marina, they were cooking lobsters in kettle drums down on the beach.

There was cause for breast-beating on our departure. We touched bottom! We also failed to heed you should never attempt to alter the scope on a dinghy painter without ensuring the bitter end is secure; the dinghy went for a sail on its own. Fortunately, the appointed spotter was able to keep it on view as we downed sail and caught up with it under engine. There followed a long and exhilarating sail of some 3.5 hours achieving 10.5 kts. We re-watered at Marina Cay at the east end of Tortola and then anchored in Trellis Bay on Beef Island for cocktails. The "rescued" dinghy was carefully used to convey us to the "Last Resort" restaurant on Bellamy Cay where we dined to music and cabaret which encompassed folk and country and western music from Roger Miller.

The next day we took in a breakfast stop at Monkey Point on Guana Island. There was no pickup buoy serving our selected mooring buoy; attempting to pick up the "eye" with the boat hook and with the boat going downwind, there was too much load on the boat hook which fell apart! Hey ho, jolly boating weather. We then had a long passage in wet and squally conditions so sought a rest anchoring for lunch off Sandy Cay which exemplified "a desert island" by comprising a single palm tree sitting on a sandy beach. From here we made passage to an anchorage in Great Harbour on Jost Van Dyke Island where bodies weary from sailing were further abused by too much food and limbo dancing at Foxy's.

After an unusual wind free peaceful night, we revisited the beautiful beach of Sandy Cay for a swim with snorkelling. We then headed for civilisation in the form of the marina at Sopers Hole, Tortola and the delights of Pusser's Landing's restaurant complex.

The cruising paradise that is the BVI none the less constantly throws up challenges. The abundance of laid moorings is such that it is easy to get caught up in them. This we did when leaving Sopers Hole. However, we readily escaped and passed between the Thatch Islands, Great and Little. We were quickly back to being involved with seamanship with an enjoyable close-hauled sail down to beautiful Cane Garden Bay with its equally beautiful beach. We rowed ashore and dined in the Paradise Club ruining legs and limbs with further limbo dancing. Guests departing the club were embarrassed to find two inebriated Brits clad in their underwear diving off the quay in pursuit of a lady's spectacles. These had been dropped off the quay while climbing into the dinghy and which were clearly visible in a torch beam lying on the bottom. Successful recovery was achieved.

Next, a beautiful sailing day. Firstly, a reach and then a series of tacks to come around the west of Tortola to Nanny Cay and then a reach south down to the Indians. We had a job setting the anchor but once secure we were rewarded with excellent snorkelling featuring fish and coral. Then it was on to the Bight on Norman Island where we picked up a mooring. We dinghied to "Willy T's", a floating bar and restaurant with good if basic food, dancing and a party atmosphere. Finding our way back to our boat in the dark was a challenge; we suspect others would have more trouble; we estimated 40 to 50 boats in the Bight.

Day 12, under sail to Deadman's Bay on Peter Island which was calm and beautiful making the business of dinghy landing that much easier. The bay had a very attractive yacht harbour and hotel surrounded by flower gardens. We motored on to another bay for our final Flotilla BBQ with the boats rafted up together. The Flotilla challenge was to write a ditty the contents of which we will spare you. We even had a Rotary Meeting since other boats as well as our two had Rotarians on board.

Our final day but the sadness reduced by a long sail before returning back to base at Maya Cove on Tortola. We anchored off "The Baths" on the southern tip of Virgin Gorda and marvelled at the pools carved out by the sea between granite boulders on the shore. The evening was occupied with preparation for our return to the UK the following day.

We took the ferry back to St Thomas and spent the day on a beach with a convenient restaurant until it was time for our evening flight back to the UK.

What can we say about our visit to the BVI? This has to be one of the most attractive cruising grounds in the world embracing as it does fantastic sailing to a host of venues with scenic beauty combined with high class facilities. Don't miss out on it.

Crew of "Dodger"

Limbo Dancing

Sandy Cay

Passage to the Baths

Preparing Lobsters <---- Anegarda > Beachcombing Sculpture

Flotilla 9
Dubrovnik, Croatia, 2008

Three years after selling our "Winkle Brig" we found ourselves on a different kind of cruise; on board the "Queen Mary 2". We visited the Caribbean and in particular the BVI where we had previously "flotillared". This invoked feelings of nostalgia and raised questions of whether we could go back to chartering and agreed it had to be flotilla sailing. The other debate was where would we go?

The following year assuaging our withdrawal symptoms we arrived in Dubrovnik to start our fourth holiday in Croatian (formerly Yugoslavian) waters. Much had happened in the intervening years with the war resulting in the division of Yugoslavia into separate countries. Hence we were in Croatia, with Sunsail on an Oceanis 323 named "Aquanut".

The authorities decreed that Sunsail had to use Croatians as lead crews. This was not wholly satisfactory; in particular the hostess lacked the necessary skills. We also queried whether our boat was fully fuelled. We were assured this was the case but later we came dangerously low on fuel in some rough weather.

Dubrovnik has been an icon of this Croatian coastline and the authorities have had to respond. Cruise liners now dock in the channel leading up to the Komolac Marina as well as being anchored off the old harbour. For us initially going north up the coast, the channel provides an easy start plus passing under a very elegant suspension bridge.

Once at sea and proceeding north west, we made passage to Sipanska Luka, a deep inlet on the south west corner of Sipan Island which runs parallel to the mainland. It was time to relax after the rigours of the journey. The following day we were up and about early and ready for the challenges of the flotilla. The day's sail was to Kobas, a delightful fishing village on the mainland peninsula running northwest towards Ston; it was an introduction to the charm of this area. We also managed a lunch stop on the north east coast of Mijet Island en route. This island runs parallel to the mainland in a NW/SE direction.

The following day we had the opportunity to explore Mijet more thoroughly by heading to Polace which sits in the Mijet National Park at the far northwest of the island. An added attraction was the ability to take a boat trip to the island of St Mary which sits in an almost landlocked lake and visit the Monastery.

Once under way from Polace, we made passage to Korcula, another island with a NW/SE orientation. Korcula town is located on the eastern tip of the island. We took dinner overlooking the sea and were entertained with a traditional show featuring a Moreska Sword Dance. We were advised this is now the only place you can see this dance performed. From Korcula, our passage enabled a lunch stop in Loviste Bay on the end of the Peljesac Peninsular followed by good sail at 5–6 knots on to Scedro on the north coast of Scedro Island.

There was a pace to the flotilla and a need not to linger on the basis there was always more to see and explore. What beckoned next was Palmizana on St Klement Island off the south coast of Hvar. We were able to dine in some style at Zori's Restaurant and also to get a taxi boat to Hvar and back the following morning. This was both sensible and enjoyable. Betting on being able to find a space in Hvar (we have done it), the odds are long. Going in on a taxi boat ensures you can explore the history and culture of the town including climbing up to the citadel from where the views are spectacular. On our return, we re-anchored in a quiet bay at the west end of St Klement Island. Mercifully we had a restful night after our busy day.

After our free sailing day, we were scheduled to reconvene with the rest of the flotilla in Vela Luka on Korcula Island. We woke up to a storm but with the necessity to meet our schedule we set out in some trepidation. We had 33 knots of wind behind us which kicked up quite a sea dousing us with salt water and we ended up with gear caked in salt; shorts would have stood up on their own! Also, our fuel gauge was indicating a worrying low level and we were concerned about the perils of arriving at Vela Luka on a tea spoonful. We radioed ahead and the lead boat came out to escort us in, then they procured containers and vehicles to fetch fuel from the nearest garage; a wonderful contrast from the surly disinterest shown us at base.

The next day, buoyed up by our achievements the previous day, we were up for a day trip out to Proizd Island at the end of the promontory jutting out to the north of Vela Luka. We anchored in the south bay and enjoyed a walk through the woods to the north bay (Batalo). Then it was back to Vela Luka to await the arrival of crews who had opted out of sailing the previous day. We anchored overnight in a bay NW of Vela Luka (Uvula Plitvine).

Despite all the diversions, momentum beckoned and the next day we were off to sea en route to Lumbarda at the other end of Korcula. Lumbarda is a wine growing area and we took a group meal in a local winery surrounded by wine casks. Throw in a nice beach and a good time was had by all.

The flotilla had been hard work and spurs had been earned. The pace slowed and we were content to relax which we did with a good sail at 8 knots. The passing ferry was entertained. We made passage to Okuklje on Mijet. A similar mood prevailed the next day as we moved on to Sudurad on the SE end of Sipon Island pausing for lunch at the end of Mijet Island. The last hop was from Sudurad to Lopud town, Lopud island, and then, after a detour to sail on past Dubrovnik, we returned to Komolac Marina. Off Dubrovnik old harbour several cruise liners and a 4- and a 5-masted schooner were anchored while tender boats buzzed about. In short, chaos.

Since Dubrovnik is a jewel not to be missed, both an evening visit by bus and a further tour the next morning were provided for us. This was a mixture of magic and nostalgia tempered by sadness. All the roofs of the buildings in Dubrovnik are red, bright and shiny with optimism. The reason is the old roofs were destroyed in the Yugoslavian war when Serbs shelled Dubrovnik from the high ground above the city. The tragedy of this war is writ large, with buildings too showing shell pocked facades. The popularity of Dubrovnik as a cruise destination brings inevitable issues; for example, if you saw a seat in a café and you wanted a coffee, grab it while you can. Patience in the presence of queues is also displayed by passengers waiting at the harbour for their lighter trips to vessels anchored off shore.

Pleasure and sadness were bedfellows as we journeyed to the airport for our flight home. The journey home was uneventful. It mattered not since nothing could steal away the notion of a location having been "well sailed". Don't miss out on your chance.

Panoramic View of Hvar from the Citadel

Flotilla 10
Paxos and Corfu, Greece, 2009

This flotilla proved to be one of the most enjoyable of our many voyages. The cruising ground offered a range of experiences including revisiting some of the jewels of the southern Ionian. From the southern Ionian, passing through the Levkas Canal, a detour into the inland sea behind Preveza with a stop at Vonitsa, then on to Lakka at the north end of Paxos, a stop on the mainland at Parga with our anchors on the beach and finally to Corfu where we were meeting friends on holiday from the UK. Amongst them was Spiro who hails from these parts so we had local knowledge as to what to see and where to take drinks and food. The authorities were also very helpful and after a bit of bureaucracy and the issue of papers we were able to take everyone for a sail. They enjoyed the sail but getting them on board from a rocky quay and between the forward guard rails proved a little awkward. On our return, a dinghy trip to the town quay was welcome.

We started our flotilla at Vounaki, as pleasant a place as any to sail from. As well as Sunsail's flotilla base, it is also their holiday base with chalets, restaurants and water sport facilities. It is a paradise for young families interested in getting out on the water offering a variety of boats and facilities together with excellent catering. A word of warning; it gets terribly hot at the height of the summer.

Berthing at Vounaki can be quite challenging which enables me to ride a hobby horse. There are two parallel quays with two rows of boats moored stern-to between them with bow anchors dropped on approach. Dropping anchors in the right place is tricky. Turning through 90 degrees onto the berth, which can be between already moored boats, while letting go ahead in the right place is difficult, particularly in a blow as the head can have a mind of its own. Holiday sailors often lack practice and heads are blown off course and anchors dropped in the wrong place. The trick is to motor in astern (the bow follows rather than veers off even in a blow) and the engine in astern acts like a stern thruster allowing a rapid turn into line. Once in line, the kedge is dropped with the bow in the right place and all attention can now be given to getting stern ropes ashore. Setting sail is also eased by no crossed anchors.

After a pleasant night making use of the resort's facilities, we were on our journey west and north to Levkas, relaxed by the thought that jewels like Abelike, Vahti and Spartakhori awaited our return. Small wonder the Onassis family have held on to their retreats at Skorpios and Skorpidhi.

Levkas was busy and we found ourselves anchored in a southerly blow with our stern facing the quay immediately below the entry to the upper part of the canal. It was a nervous night but we were humbled by the sight on an adjacent boat of a chap sailing with his girlfriend, who once moored up, relaxed by detaching his artificial leg. We were storm bound in Levkas through the following day, it being judged that exiting through the floating bridge into the uncertain depths of the exit channel presented too much of a risk. It did avail us of a walk around the town and also an impressive sunset with the sun disappearing into the low-lying land to the west.

Fortunately, the following morning brought better conditions and the flotilla was able to make its way through the floating swing bridge and out through a complex but buoyed channel. The wind was still very boisterous and along with others we preferred to motor. It is a short hop from Levkas to the mouth of the "Inland Sea" (Amvrakikos Kolpos) and the pleasant resort of Vonitsa with its Venetian Fort. There were impressive views from the Fort and the town had a balanced ambience from an attractive busy waterfront with restaurants adjacent to the quay side to rustic slopes hosting cacti. The cacti prickles appeared to present little defence to foraging tortoises! After an overnight stay in Vonitsa, we had a great sail back to the port of Preveza. The quay side was very crowded and we had to squeeze bow first in between two yachts which were stern to. Then we were at last able to sail on to Lakka a large bay at the north end of Paxos Island. But more about Lakka later.

The following day gave us a cloudless sky and light winds. We spent the day motoring down the west coast of Paxos marvelling at the many inlets and caves set into a range of white cliffs. Some of the cliffs project out from the island and at sea level caves have been worn right through the projections.

The lead boat took us back south to Gaios; what was on offer was a night on the tiles eating, drinking and dancing. The skipper clearly had local associations and the promised night on the tiles lived up to expectation and much merrymaking ensued. Gaios is an attractive place situated in the channel which lies between Paxos and the off shore island of Ay Nikolaos. It is well sheltered and very popular with a large number of boats moored on both sides of the channel. While navigating up the channel vigilance is required; tripper ferries claim right of way. En route to Gaios we took the opportunity of a lunch time stop at a bay on the north east corner of Anti Paxos where the water is an unbelievable turquoise colour. Backed by olive groves it was a beautiful place.

The next day, more merrymaking was on the agenda, this time in Mongonisi, a beach a short distance away from Gaios and on the south east corner of Paxos. The boats were rafted up with bow anchors and stern lines for a traditional flotilla barbecue. These events are usually great fun since by this time people have got to know one another. The relaxed firelight atmosphere helps to enhance a flotilla ambience.

Now we really had to get on with heading north and course was set for Parga on the mainland. Here on a gently shelving sandy beach the flotilla was secured for the night by running into very shallow water and the anchors being manually run up the beach and dug in. Meanwhile kedges from the stern were laid out by dinghy. On a lightly shelving beach with good holding in sand, it is an effective way to raft up boats. The beach was just north of the town of Parga which was a short but hilly walk over a promontory to the restaurants in the town. A delightful place to be moored and sustained.

The next stop on the itinerary was Corfu but many of the other flotilla crews had other ideas. Having lost a day storm bound in Levkas they were anxious to get back to explore the Southern Ionian rather than take the long passage to Corfu and back. However, having made arrangements to meet friends in Corfu we needed to continue. So the lead boat, ourselves and one other boat went on to Corfu while the others all turned back. It worked out very well; we were introduced to Corfu and our friends got to have a sail. The wind was a little light but better this than half a gale. Our trips to a rooftop bar for aperitifs and a restaurant where Spiro's hand was warmly shaken were great and it was fun introducing our friends to sailing. Now all we had to do was to get back to Vounaki.

We left Corfu and the wind picked up and we had a splendid sail back to Lakka. It is a charming place, spacious and scenic with attractive restaurants ashore. It holds a special place in our hearts in as much that we had or were achieving one part of what we had set out to do on this trip i.e. to sail to Corfu and meet our friends. We had some wine to celebrate. Now it was all about the return journey, first to Levkas and the canal and then to meet our second objective which was to revisit some of the jewels of the Southern Ionian.

We managed to make Levkas in time to pass through the floating bridge; in fact, we were circling around for some time. Then through the canal and we were free and determined to make the best of being in our beloved Ionian. We had a gentle sail down past Nidri and into the magic of Vlikho bay with its space and its restaurants. We stayed the night having had a romantic meal on board. Next day we proceeded down the Meganisi Channel taking lunch off Thilia Island. We nosed into Spartakhori (Spiglia) but it was too windy to anchor and be able to climb up to the village. Having parked this option, plan B was to carry on into Abelike Bay where we anchored with a stern line ashore. With limited space and still very windy we elected not to stay the night but instead to compromise and settled on Vahti. We had done a quick tour of our beloved Southern Ionian but a combination of wind and lack of space had thwarted our dream. It only remained for us to take lunch the following morning at Ormos Varko on the mainland en route to Vounaki.

All in all, this was a very enjoyable experience particularly going north from the Levkas canal. Sadly, dreams don't last for ever and the Southern Ionian, like many others, is succumbing to popularity and so loses some of its initial charm.

Flotilla Convoy through the Levkas Canal

91

Dancing in Gaios

Beach BBQ

Beach anchoring at Parga

Flotilla 11
Orhaniye, Turkey, 2010

The flotilla commenced at the Sunsail base in Orhaniye which lies to the south at the head of the Hisaronic Channel running up the south side of the Datcha Peninsula. Our boat was a Beneteau 321 called "Celeste". Orhaniye was a small bay with wooden piers in front of the restaurant which could accept the flotilla stern to with bow anchors. After Skipper's briefing, we set sail for Dirsek which lies close to Cape Apostoli on the south side of the Hisaronic Channel. We had a great beam sail to Dirsek which turned out to be a small pleasant north facing bay with a concrete quay at its head backed by a flower and flag bedecked taverna building. The quay was ample enough to comfortably accommodate the flotilla stern to. We were also able to walk up the right-hand coast to bays providing pleasant anchoring sites to other boats. We went straight into fellowship mood with a punch party. There may have been a few sore heads at Skipper's briefing the next morning which was held on the quay.

The next morning provided us with a piece of sailing which we will always remember with pride. En route to Simi, our next port of call, we again had a beam reach during which we set up for zero rudder. In other words, we adjusted the main and jib sheets so that we didn't need to tend the rudder which remained amidships and imposed no drag on our forward motion. We sailed faster than anyone else. The other duty we had to perform on board was to lower the Turkey courtesy pennant and to hoist a Greek one as we approached Simi.

Simi Town is one of the jewels in this part of the world. It has a narrow harbour and the town itself rises steeply from the foreshore. One problem in lying to a bow anchor with a stern line ashore was the need to drop the bow anchor just astern of the boats on the opposite quay. We are not sure if we did well or were lucky to avoid any interference. The winding paths to the top pass through elegant homes, shops and churches affording spectacular views of the harbour below. There were also a range of local ware on offer in the shops including sponges; sponge fishing is a local industry. The piece de resistance of the day was a lamb pie to die for. Simi lived up to its reputation.

Next morning, we reluctantly focused on the passage to Panormitis, a bay on the southern tip of Simi Island. En route we took in a lunchtime stop in an arid bay with very little vegetation. Then it was on to Panormitis itself and we anchored in the bay. The most conspicuous feature is the St Michael's Monastery (St Michael is the patron saint of seafarers) which is a long white building fronting the shore. There is also a conspicuous windmill which overlooks the harbour. We enjoyed a magnificent sun-set, the sun sinking into the mouth of the bay. The monastery tower was also lit up.

We couldn't leave the next day without a visit to the monastery. On eventually leaving the bay, we shed a fan belt while under engine in somewhat swelly conditions. After an hour with my head in the engine compartment, I'd given it my best and we radioed for the flotilla engineer. After another hour, we were Bristol fashion thanks to the skill and expedience of our engineer. There is a message here and that is that flotillas are a wonderful way of going to sea with a safety blanket wrapped around you. Then it was back into Turkish waters and an anchorage in Bozburun. The town lies at the head of an open bay with a very rocky shoreline. On approach, the most conspicuous feature is a mosque which is the central feature of a town which spreads out along the waterfront. It is a diverting place with cafes, carpet shops and restaurants. We rested here ahead of our period of free sailing.

Our free time took us first to Bozuc Buku; now more often referred to as Loryma. The bay is somewhat open and has a very rocky ambience which lacks the charm of more wooded slopes. There are remnants of an ancient citadel on the port side of the entrance. We moored at the head of the bay stern to a wooden jetty with fore and aft lines provided by the restaurant where we dined. The whole ambience was one of 'making do with what we have' but for all that they looked after us very well.

The second leg of our free time was to Gerbekse Cove on the east side of the Karaburan peninsula. This was a delightful place with the presence of turquoise water adding to the ambience of the usual rocky shore backed by trees and bushes. We moored stern to the shore with our own lines sharing the ambience with a number of gulets cruising out of Marmaris. It was tempting to use the dinghy to go and socialise but typical English reserve kicked in. We were also able to walk along the shore peeping out between the rocks before leaving. Reunion with the flotilla beckoned the next day and we set sail to Ciftlik.

We re-joined the flotilla at Ciftlik and were the guests of the Kumlubuku Yacht Club. What a place! From the natural beauty of the various bays we had visited, this was luxury on a grand scale. A turquoise pool was surrounded by terraces and colour filled gardens and loungers which were bed sized with white bed type mattresses. Not only this, but throngs of vegetation hung down over your pitch to provide shade and privacy. We called them "hairy huts".

Our next port of call was Ekincik which lies on the mainland coast just east of Marmaris. It is a classic horseshoe bay with a nook in the south east corner which is protected from the south. There is a small marina here developed by the "My Marina" restaurant. The restaurant is high up on the headland providing the protection. You can approach it via a steep path or alternatively there is a quaint chair lift. It is a great place to eat with spectacular views.

The next day's option was a real opportunity. We were able to take a boat trip up the Dalyan River to the ruins of ancient Caunus with its amphitheatre and remains of mosaic floors. We had great fun feeding a giant turtle as we progressed through reedy shallows. We continued upstream passing rock tombs elaborately carved into the cliffs above. It was a very diverting experience. After our boat trip, we returned to "Celeste" and anchored in Bay Kargi Koyu SSW of Ekincik.

Time was running out so it was post haste to return to Gerbekse Cove which exists courtesy of a low spit of land which isolates it from an adjacent bay and provides shelter from the east. There are ancient ruins and a Byzantyne church on the isthmus. We anchored close to the beach with a sternline to the beach to allow us to pull along the rope to reach the shore. The bay was popular during the day with gulets from Marmaris but was quiet overnight.

We moved on to Loryma at the end of the Karaburun peninsula. This is a large bay open to a southerly swell and the holding not good. There are ruins of ancient Loryma along the shore. None the less we anchored comfortably below the Citadel close to the "Sailors House" restaurant. Here we held the traditional cocktail competition followed by the model "potato" boat race; ours did very well.

After a calm and relaxing night, the next morning we were treated to fresh baked bread from a rock oven on the beach. Then we were off to be challenged with winds gusting to force 8 en route to Kocabahce which lies opposite Koca Island between Dirsek and Selimiye. We were close hauled under reefed main and headsail and it was very bumpy. We were pleased to arrive at the "Sailors Paradise" restaurant in Kocabahce tired but very satisfied.

Alas the following day saw us making passage back to Orhaniye. Flotilla last days are very often awkward days since the focus of the base is getting the boats ready for the next crews rather than taking care of the departing ones. On this occasion, we were taken to the Marti Marina and Hotel just up the coast which was a very nice place to await arrival of our bus to the airport. Satisfaction in our boat handling and the fellowship of other crews enhanced a relaxed mood.

Simi Lamb Pie

Line ashore – Gerbekse Cove

Luxury loungers at Kumlubuku Yacht Club

Quaint chair lift to "My Marina" restaurant, Ekincik

Flotilla 12
Southern Ionian, Greece, 2011

Having spent time in the Southern Ionian in 1983 and again in 1985 and at the end of the Northern Ionian flotilla to Paxos and Corfu in 2009, we wanted very much to revisit this very attractive area. Hence, we found ourselves at Vounaki, at that time owned by Sunsail as a shore-based holiday complex as well as a flotilla base, joining a flotilla which was to sail around the Southern Ionian.

Vounaki is an excellent flotilla base with facilities ashore to ensure any issues, boat or people, which arise can readily be dealt with. The mooring facilities comprise two long pontoons some 50 metres apart; bow anchors are dropped midway between the pontoons and craft motor astern to tie up to them. This greatly assists the access of both crews arriving and boat yard staff dealing with servicing and safety issues.

As well as the boat, the weather and the cruising ground, a key aspect of success is the flotilla leader. We were lucky enough to have Rob Belsey as our leader; he was a consummate sailor and we learned a lot from him.

We enjoyed a pleasant beam reach against a stunning mountainous backing as we made our way to Ormos Vlikho, a large but sheltered bay protected by a promontory which lies just south of Nidri, Levkas island. There was ample room to anchor with depths from 3 to 5 metres away from the shore. However, it was very blustery when we arrived making anchoring quite difficult; we re-laid the anchor 3 times before we were satisfied it was well bedded in. As soon as the sun dipped behind the mountain the wind suddenly died as if a switch had turned it off! We enjoyed a calm evening and this is probably the default pattern in this area. There were tavernas ashore; Dimitris is the most conspicuous but the Taverna Gialos is adjacent.

We woke early enjoying the blissful weather and an absolute glassy calm but it was time to make passage. We had a pleasant sail down the east coast of Levkas leaving the island of Meganisi to port; our destination the busy port of Sivota located at the southern end of Levkas. It was much busier than on our previous visits when this was the flotilla base and Yannis was the only taverna but we were still able to moor stern-to outside Yannis. A good night was had by all.

Such is the ambience of Southern Ionian life that it is difficult to galvanise oneself into moving on the next day but moving on we must. This time we were bound for Ayios Eufimia which lies between Sami and Fiskardo on the east coast of northern Cephalonia. This passage between Ithaca and Cephalonia is open to both northerly and southerly winds and can be boisterous. Initially we met only 16Kts and had a downwind reach of 5Kts. Gradually the wind increased and it took a broach to waken us up to sailing more cautiously. We had the second reef in with a windspeed of 19kts. Further into the channel, the conditions were more benign.

Ay Eufimia offers the chance to anchor; it is prudent to see your anchor is well dug in. Alternatively moor stern to on either the northern quay or the eastern quay when tripper boats have departed. You can also take a swim off a rocky promontory which projects into the harbour at the south east point. A conspicuous tree with foliage outcrops, nicknamed the "hat stand" tree on previous visits, marked the limit of our exploratory walk.

It was time to move on to Vahti on Ithaca Island. We refer to it as "big" Vahti to distinguish it from "little" Vahti which is on Meganisi. En route to Vahti you pass an attractive white chapel which is situated on Point Andreou. There is a bay to the north east of the town which offers good holding and all-round shelter. The bay is fringed by white rocks with green vegetation above and turquoise shallow water close in shore which demands a swim much enjoyed by all members of the flotilla. It becomes a bit repetitive to say again what a delightful spot this is but this is the nature of the Southern Ionian.

The next place up was Frikes, which again has seen tourist development in recent years. At the time of our visit, tourism was limited to beaches being used as family camp sites with accommodation provided either in tents or in beached boats. Shangri La takes all sorts of routes.

Then, rounding the north of Ithaca, we head for Fiskardo; a great place to chill out. It was a field of delights from cobble streets rising up the hill between brightly coloured buildings with balconies, bays to swim in and flora offering shade. Conveniently, the flotilla was lying from bow anchors with sterns on the quay and "The Captain's Cabin" was the place to be seen so we went to the place to be seen and had a nice dinner. You look out on craft from local fishermen to "Mr Bigs" frantically looking for somewhere to park large motor cruisers.

There is no peace for the committed flotilla sailor. Our next port of call was that of Kioni on the island of Ithaca, again with the opportunity to have stern lines to the quay, though to find depth we had to use the dinghy between boat and shore. The waterfront was buzzing with attractions ranging from souvenir shops displaying goods in attractive timber cabinets, olive oil being sold from large flagons and gnarled trees. Facilities were no longer primitive as experienced on our previous visits; gone was the "Green Door".

It was in Kioni that Rob Belsey gave us good advice about arriving at a quay or an anchorage in a blow or in a crowded location. Approach in reverse; your engine and rudder act as stern thrusters giving you control of your course astern and the mast and bow are bound to follow. In a blow if you approach going ahead, your mast can easily be blown off.

Port Leone on Kalamos was now beckoning with the promise of the flotilla BBQ which was the usual 'it can't get much better than this' event. It included a cocktail competition with promotional poem and a "fire dance" by the flotilla engineer Matt. Port Leone was abandoned by its inhabitants after the 1953 earthquake which destroyed the water supply. Ruined houses, olive presses and cisterns give a deserted air to the place. However, the church with its ornamental screens and oil lamps is still looked after by a few villagers from Kalamos town.

The next day was the day I lost the race round Kalamos Island. We were the smallest boat and we were leading. En route to Port Kalamos, I was preoccupied with steering to get out of the wind shadow from Kastos (the wind was westerly) rather than steering the shortest course. It cost us dear and we had to settle for second place. Port Kalamos is the main port on Kalamos and the quay and its surrounding buildings reflected this; none the less the contrast between white buildings and summer blooms is ever present. One of the last trading caiques in the Ionian can be seen in the harbour.

Abelike Bay, a favourite from the past, beckoned. Once a place to swing, now there is not room for everyone and anchoring with a stern line ashore is essential. Still we enjoyed a peaceful evening and reminisced with fond memories of our previous visits when our flotilla was the sole occupant of the bay and the location of great BBQs.

Our last port of call was to Vahti on Meganisi. There can always be a sting in the tail and we had it. We had a windy passage which included altering course away from a ferry. However once in "little" Vahti with the now familiar blooms and stalls we recovered our poise. Poise was important since, on arrival back at Vounaki, we had arranged with Sunsail for both Valerie and I to take our International Certificates of Competency; we both passed. Rob Belsey's stewardship during the flotilla helped by crew mate Jill was valuable to us.

Adieu to the Southern Ionian. We came with a passion; we returned with the passion intact.

Morning Calm in Ormos Vlikho

"Hat Stand" tree Ay Eufimia

Traditional trading caique in Kalamos port

More BBQ fun

ICC success for us and 2 other flotilla members

Flotilla 13
Northern Aegean, Greece, 2013

This cruising ground begs a visit by the intriguing shape of the Halkidhiki Peninsulas and in part sailing under the shadow of Mount Athos. Impressive as the latter is as a backdrop, it can result in strong downwinds round the ends of the Peninsulas. Also, for those wishing to visit the Monasteries on Akti, the procedure tends to be lengthy and bureaucratic and, at the time of our visit, women were not permitted ashore. There is no public access to Akti. Having said all that, there are sufficient attractive boltholes to ride out strong winds. The cruising ground offers variety from mainland ports to small local harbours, deep and beautiful sheltered bays and interesting features such as a canal transit. To do justice to the area in a relatively short time, daily distances can be quite long (c 25 nautical miles) but with summer winds rated at force 4, it is relaxing sailing though boisterous near the peninsula heads.

We set off from the Neilson base at Nea Skioni on the south coast of the Kassandra Peninsula, in a Beneteau 325 named "Amanda". Our first port of call was Porto Koufo on the extreme south west tip of Sinthonia, the middle peninsular of the three that comprise Halkidhiki.

Next stop was Sikias on the eastern side of the peninsular where we were rafted up off a small beach with a taverna. Then a good gentle sail to Panayia accompanied by a pod of dolphins.

Each flotilla has lessons to learn; in our case we touched bottom on two occasions. On the first occasion, we accepted an allocated berth alongside the quay at Panayia without question and a second larger boat came and moored alongside us. The following morning found both boats aground. Instead of retiring to a café until the tide came back, there followed a master class on techniques for re-floating a grounded boat. Kedges were laid out, halyards were hauled from the quay and weight in the form of bodies was placed right forward and then right aft. All to no avail until the tide came in. Perhaps the most embarrassing aspect of this incident was that for much of the time we were being watched by those coming and going in a sizeable "Pirate" tripper boat moored stern-to adjacent to us. These privations did not occupy us for long since once we had floated off and escaped the harbour, we had a delightful passage down to Nisis Dhiaporos.

It really doesn't get much better than this place. That evening; we shared it with one other boat anchored a fair way from us. We were surrounded by islands and small hills, green but with trees and rocks. When at sea looking ashore, as the sun goes down shadows lengthen and the shore takes on a mystical three-dimensional aspect of light, shadow and colour. You can often see this but this evening in the Kriftos Bay at Nisis Dhiaporos it was very special.

Next day we had a great sail across the Gulf of Singitiki to Ammouliani Island and thence to Pirgadhikia. This small village situated at the head of the Gulf is a delightful place with buildings clinging to the hillside and the views overlooking the Gulf make the climb to the top of the village well worthwhile. It was then back to Porto Koufo.

Porto Koufo is a wonderful natural harbour offering (normally) all-round shelter with both quays and good holding ground. We did a beach anchor here, reminiscent of that we did in Parga on an earlier flotilla. The bow anchor is dropped on the beach and then manually run ashore while a kedge is laid aft with the boat between the two. Sadly, a local resident took exception to our presence and called the authorities; we had to leave. Our lead crew nobly moved most of the yachts to the quayside at the head of the harbour while we all indulged in a meal at the local taverna. Just as well, since we had a heavy blow all through the next day with gusts of 25 knots. A few of the crews had elected to anchor in the bay just inside the mouth but next morning joined us seeking the security of the quayside.

Following the storm, we had a rough passage to Koutsoupia Beach, on the west coast of Sinthonia. Here we rafted up then went ashore for a group meal with much camaraderie.

Our next destination was the resort of Nikitas. En route we circumnavigated the Island of Kelifos which, from the south, looks like a giant turtle. Nikitas is a small resort with a long sandy beach backed by a string of restaurants and cafes. However, we were puzzled that these were largely unpopulated. One explanation may be that the accommodation in the area is taken up by tour companies from

Bulgaria and Russia which are all done on an all-inclusive basis, hence there are fewer diners eating out.

Another place worth visiting was Nea Fokaia with its conspicuous Byzantine tower and its underground church. The harbour is in a fair-sized curved bay and shallow which allows easy mooring. Here was held a traditional flotilla competition: model boat racing. We took the prize for the first model yacht to reach the opposite side of the harbour.

Other highlights included navigating the Portas Canal which in fact renders the Kassandra Peninsula an "island". We did this in convoy and a decree by the flotilla skipper that we should dress in roman togas provided an additional diversion.

Our final destination was Nea Moudhania busy with commerce rather than tourism. At the time of our visit, the town showed signs of the then current Greek austerity with many shops closed and shuttered. A prominent feature was an elaborate brick-built Church.

The second time we touched bottom was a classic. Nea Moudhania was busy and we were directed to berth to seaward of the commercial quay. We were tight in with boats both ahead and astern of us. We had a headwind the next morning and it was difficult to slip bow and stern lines and to move the bow out without the risk of touching the boat ahead or astern. As soon as the bow pointed clear of the boat ahead, we successfully gunned our way out. Getting bow and stern lines inboard without getting anything round the prop became the pre-occupation and we overlooked that we still had forward momentum. As we turned off the wind there was a slight bump and rumble from forward (we could now clearly see the bottom!). It was a gentle bump but instructive. Whatever other pre-occupations you may have, having enough water is pre-eminent.

Then it was a long rough haul back to base in Nea Skioni. Summing up, the cruising ground offers plenty of opportunity to sail both well and comfortably and offers a variety of experiences from some mainland sophistication to romantic retreats.

Group meal at Koutsoupia Beach

Convoy through the Portas Canal

Model Boats ready for the "off"

and the winners

Flotilla 14
Peloponnese, Greece, 2014

The Saronic Gulf and the water which lies to the east of the Peloponnisos peninsula have to be one of the most idyllic cruising grounds for both large and small craft. However, the idyll comes at a cost as the proximity of Athens produces a lot of boats, some of them of a significant size. To a large extent, providing navigation is carried out with respect for all, then there is room for all. The twin terror of a large boat navigating an attractive but small bay with no regard for others let alone the rule of the road seems inevitable. The old cliché 'I don't believe it' at times will be heard. Enough negatives; this area still remains a gem.

We went as a couple but with advancing years, we were now in our seventies, it was prudent and indeed enjoyable to sail with a Neilson Flotilla. We had the twin benefits of a very competent lead crew and a lively group of fellow sailors. Our yacht was a Beneteau 331 named "Portia".

The starting point was Navplion which is located at the north eastern head of the Argolic Gulf. It boasts modern marina facilities complimented by narrow streets with hidden local and bijou restaurants. The town nestles under the rocky Akronauplia Peninsula and is dominated by the Venetian Palamidi fortress. We set off in perfect sailing weather and in no time at all were anchored in the quiet and peaceful ambience of Vivari (Khaidhari) on the east side of the Argolic Gulf. Here the rigours of the journey from the UK are soon forgotten.

The following day our destination was Porto Kheli, in an almost land locked cove some 20 miles to the south. Small as the cove was, all the boats were stern-to a quay which gave the flotilla fellowship a head start. We did not know it at this stage but the charm of this place was repeated in almost all the places we visited.

Time to relax and swim in the heat of the day is appreciated and we were afforded this next day in Ormos Skindos on the north of Dhokos Island. It was our own rock fringed turquoise swimming pool with an inviting temperature. From here we moved on to Ermioni, a bustling town with good berthing facilities, again stern to the quay on the north side of the town, and with attractive gardens, fruit and flower shops and restaurants ashore. The contrast between our busy morning activity and the relaxed mode of the evening was quite significant.

The next morning's briefing on the quay and an intervention by ourselves caused some hilarity. The flotilla leader was advising us not to go into Hydra Harbour as it is crammed with commercial traffic but instead to anchor in the adjacent Mandraki Bay. He showed us a briefing map which had a large hook in the middle of the Bay. We could not resist explaining that the hook was highly significant since we had spent our honeymoon in Mandraki Bay 47 years previously. So we got to anchor in Mandraki Bay and albeit much busier, it did not appear to have changed markedly. To have stayed overnight would have filled hankies with tears of nostalgia, but hey this was a flotilla and we were off again bound for the diversions of Poros. Outside Hydra we were overtaken by a very large hydrofoil travelling at speed. From our deck level she looked very menacing but surprisingly she created very little wake riding on her foils.

Poros has and has had diversions a plenty. Poros opposed the Government at the end of the Greek War of Independence and blew up two government ships in the process. Today it is a busy and diverting place. The town is built on the rocky slopes of the small volcanic peninsular and a must is to climb to the summit at which a large Greek flag flies proudly.

Following briefing the next morning we were off to the north to visit Epidaurus with divided opinions as to its distractions. The first of these was a punch party on the beach on the evening we arrived with prizes available for the best concoctions. More seriously was the opportunity to visit the amphitheatre on the following morning. Valerie had been there before we were married and stressed I should not miss it. It was an extraordinary achievement to build such a structure with the techniques which were available at the time. As I did in the theatre at Knidos in Turkey, I could not resist rendering Hamlet's soliloquy much to the curiosity of passers-by. This doubtful incident apart, it proved to be a wonderful day out.

Now afternoon, it was time to move on again, this time to an overnight anchorage in a light southerly at Dhorousa off the west coast of Angistri Island. There were a number of different boats strung out with plenty of space between us; this and a balmy evening gave an ambience of it being a special place.

This was rudely displaced the following morning when we moved on to the bay atop of Moni Island. It was here we witnessed the extraordinary scene of two very large motor cruisers dropping their anchors at the shallower east end of the bay and then laying back on their anchors so that they sealed off the bay to other craft. The smaller vessel had taken up this position when the larger vessel parked alongside causing umbrage in the inner vessel who took up his chain and departed. During these manoeuvres and even after them with one chain stretching to an anchor in relatively shallow water, even dinghies were unable to enter the bay. There needs to be a system where such arrogance is reported. From the distance at which we were constrained, the bay looked delightful with facilities clearly visible on the shore.

Then it was post haste to Methana on the east coast of the Methana Peninsula. It has something of a blemished reputation since there can be hydrogen sulphide gas emanating from the sulphur baths. We were not so afflicted and the place was pleasant enough with arched buildings and a bell tower with three bells.

It was time now for us to retrace our way a) through the diverting Poros Channel and b) to revisit the pleasant ambience of Ermioni where this time we moored along the quay on the south side of the town. Then to Ormos Zoyioryia, a beautiful bay on the north west corner of Spetsai island, where we were to build the traditional Flotilla raft with all boats anchored side by side. There followed the traditional beach barbecue but I was denied by circumstance from singing "Younger than Springtime are You" to the Flotilla Hostess. She, poor sole, was later hoisted up her mast in a bosun's chair.

We were now nearing the end of our cruise but still had the opportunity to visit the eastern coast of the Peninsula, firstly at Plaka (Leonidhion) with an unprepossessing restaurant but with a fine view from its dining terrace. We then goosewinged up the coast past three conspicuous windmills to Tiros. Before this passage an edict had been issued that only females were allowed to helm; we suddenly seemed to have quite a few tall strong ladies whose dress suggested a sudden onset of butchiness. Tiros was our last waterfront town of the cruise and it was pleasant enough with tavernas and cafes along the waterfront.

The penultimate leg was to Koiladhia, a north facing bay half way up the Argolic Gulf. This is a charming place with mooring available at pontoons and plenty of relatively shallow water to anchor in, though the shallows extend someway from the shore. There were also redundant moorings which needed avoiding. We opted to anchor and enjoyed an amazing sunset with the sun setting behind mainland mountains of 1000m. I was nervous and with good reason.

The sun beating down on high mainland peaks heats the air considerably during the day. At sunset and at altitude, the air cools down rapidly, is heavier than the lower air and rolls off the mountain as a katabatic wind, typically at Force 6. Mercifully the anchor held though we yawed about through an arc of 120 degrees through much of the night.

Finally, we returned to base at Navplion. We couldn't leave without visiting the Citadel so despite the afternoon heat ("Mad dogs and Englishmen…"), we climbed the winding track of about 1000 steps. We were greatly rewarded by the superb views over the Argolic Gulf and a tour of the Fort. The day ended with a final crew dinner, then, very regretfully, it was time for the plane home.

As indicated earlier, this area has an enormous amount to offer both in sailing waters and historical points of call. It is however busy and although our experience is that yachtsmen generally behave responsibly, we did witness incidents where manners not to mention the rule of the road were flouted.

Skipper's Briefing

Amphitheatre at Epidaurus

Traditional BBQ

Female Skippers?!

Flotilla 15
Marmaris to Kas, Turkey, 2015

Picture if you will the opportunity to sail downwind for 14 days in attractive sailing waters without the responsibility of having to turn round and sail 14 days upwind to return to where you started. This opportunity presented itself in the summer of 2015 when Neilsons were offering a flotilla which took you from Marmaris to Kas along the Lycian coast. The coast line is attractive to both conventional tourists and to yachtsmen in as much that it offers deserted bays, holiday resorts and an interesting history. Remnants from historical times are found along the coast. The flotilla got off to a good start since on the short shuttle boat trip from Marmaris town to the marina, situated on the island of Nimara Adasi, we were embraced from behind by the ample figure of Bruno, a big man with a big heart who we had met on a previous flotilla. Unknowingly, he and I had lived within 100 yards or so in the same area of Birmingham. I hailed from Scotland and he from Italy and such is the brotherhood of sailing, we had ended up in Greece on a previous flotilla trying to refloat grounded boats (see Halkidhiki Flotilla).

Choosing a flotilla base which is also a shore-based holiday centre greatly aids the difficult business of getting up to 40 or so people sorted into a dozen or so boats. The range of facilities at the Adakoy holiday base centre made this a lot easier. So after a restaurant meal and a sleep on our boat, a Dufour 35' named "Kilifi", we were all set the next morning for our first port of call at Ekincik.

Ekincik is a delightful wooded cove which we had visited on an earlier flotilla. Again we made use of the small "marina" provided by the restaurant "My Marina". Unfortunately, the lift to the restaurant, used by a disabled lady on our earlier visit, no longer functions. However, the quality of the food and the views were sufficient incentive to climb the hill to the restaurant.

Our next few days provided both delightful light wind sails and equally delightful anchorages on the west side of Skopea Limani. There is a wide range of anchorages in the main bay and we chose to overnight in Wall Bay where there is both a quay and a restaurant. This is archetypical of the area, a delightful combination of ambience and facilities. We paid the area further homage by taking a lunch time stop, this time in Round Bay, before sailing on to Tomb Bay. This is aptly named since within a short walk over uneven ground, there are burial chambers cut into the rocky face. There is also a handy restaurant actually sitting on the beach surrounded by trees in blossom which made for an idyllic evening. There was no doubt that the crab meat was fresh, the crabs are harvested from pens at the water's edge. There is also envy in a place like this since as you walk along the shore, you find locally owned yachts afloat in clefts in the rocks which provide secure berths much like you would find in a marina. Oh, for a second life where you could inhabit gems like this rather than worrying about the mortgage on a 3 up and 3 down.

After the natural and isolated jewels of the Skopea Limani it was time to return to civilisation and to make passage to Gocek. We were in the Skopea Marina in Gocek which offered an attractive room in which to dine and also to have Skipper's briefing the following morning. The room overlooked an azure blue rectangular swimming pool.

The south west passage from Gocek to Fethiye passes a string of islands which provide ready way marks. Despite much of the town having been destroyed by an earthquake in 1957, Fethiye has recovered well. Fethiye is heavily dependent on the gulet trade and we can imagine that contemporary issues with Turkish holidays will have had a big effect. We were based in what is now the Moorings Base with scallop shaped pools, bars shaded under palms, tables shaded by overhanging thatch and decking along the waterfront. A run ashore was well worthwhile for no other reason than to see fresh produce displayed in local delicatessen, good quality souvenir shops and bars to tempt you for another beer. However, the following day was a day and a night stop to do as were wont, so after Skipper's briefing, we were off to sea with the promise of an overnight anchorage in picturesque and quiet Round Bay which we had pencilled in at our earlier lunch stop. It rewarded us with a night as if in a mill pond. Other crews in the flotilla, tempted by the enthusiasm of the skipper, elected to experience paragliding from Babadag Mountain. It sounded exciting but a bit risky at this early stage of the holiday.

From Round Bay, it was on to Karacaoren, a quiet unspoiled bay tucked in behind a promontory jutting out into the bay south of the island of Gemiler Adasi and protected from the east by the island of Karacaoren Adalari. It is a peaceful spot to anchor which was not spoiled by the rather quirky conspicuous restaurant close to the beach. It proved a convenient stop on our passage south to Kalkan. A long passage, 31nm, required that we got underway early and set a course for Kalkan where we had the chance to enjoy a quayside mooring. The place is an attractive blend of traditional buildings, mosques and minarets, tourist shops but also a character of its own with hilly retreats and a lively waterfront.

The next day involved a short hop to Kas where again we moored at the town quay and in part began an exploration of the town. However, our focus was on the morrow where we were expecting very strong winds on a 20nm. downwind sail to Polemos. We retired early and early the next day we anchored in Bayindir Limani for the express purpose of tying down the second reef of the mainsail absolutely flat. We didn't want to have to do this under way; it was prudent seamanship but it left us with the mindset that we would sail under main. We experienced winds of 38 knots and a boat speed of 6.8 knots through the water. Our course speed was quite slow since the weather helm to keep the boat from rounding up during gusts was considerable. We needed to gybe but were frightened of doing so or of luffing into the swell. It was hairy and all because we kept the main up (it was after all reefed down tight) when we could and should have had a comfortable sail under genoa. I was relieved to see the boat ahead gybe safely and we followed suit. Later in the bar I explained how relieved we were to see his precautionary gybe – it turned out his gybe was accidental and uncontrolled! It was hairy out there.

Our adventure was not over; to reach Polemos Buki from Kekova Roads we had to turn into the wind and under engine to stem a considerable swell to reach the quay and taverna at the west end of the Roads. Never has a quay or a beer been more welcome. And here beginneth the lesson, never pre-select your sail plan until you get out there. That there were historic ruins worth visiting from Polemos Buku was a good enough excuse to stay in Polemos through the following day.

Now we were a long way east, and downwind, of Kas Marina where our cruise was to end, so plans needed laid to achieve our return. We had been told we could not leave Kekova Roads without a visit to Gokkaya Limani. This we did admiring the castle at Kale Koy and then we returned for a merciful peaceful overnight anchorage in Ucagiz Limani. In the interests of arriving back at our final destination we set off early the next morning and since our course was upwind, we motored all the way. This gave us some relaxation time which we spent in a second visit to Bayindir Limani, just south of Kas Marina. Our Gods were with us and we spent our final hours before returning to base in the company of a turtle who was far from camera shy.

Such an unusual flotilla needs a few concluding remarks. Never take a downwind passage for granted. We, who boast that a boat is fastest and safest when it is balanced to sail itself with no hand on the tiller, committed ourselves to a course of action where hauling the boat off the wind to prevent her rounding into irons needed full rudder. When you are at sea, you are always at school.

This flotilla was run by Neilsons and their boats and service were excellent. It was particularly nice to start a flotilla in a base which is also a holiday base; victualling and boat maintenance is easier to organise. A plea on their behalf. This cruising ground has many rock fringed bays where anchoring is a delight. A member of our flotilla lost an anchor, and therefore also the chain back to the anchor locker shackle, jammed under a rock whose precise location was not conspicuously marked and could not be subsequently found. On behalf of all charterers, please buoy your anchor.

Neil embraced by mate Bruno

Crabs for supper!

Spice shop in Fethiye

Tombs at Polemos

Castle at Kale Koy

Flotilla 16
Sporades Islands and the Gulf of Volos, Greece, 2016

It is said of life that you should never repeat something which was a rewarding experience. It is also held that if you sail in Greece in July you are likely to experience meltemi winds. However, in 2016 we found ourselves pre-occupied in June with our Golden Wedding celebrations to the extent that we were not able to sail until later. Furthermore, we had set our hearts on returning to the Sporades Islands haunted by the beauty of the sun setting in Panormou Bay. So plans were made, notwithstanding my having had knee replacement surgery at the turn of the year!

Since we had to book at short notice, the only flotilla operator who could accommodate us uses a model which is different to most others in that they book the charters and organise the flotilla while the boats are supplied and maintained by a different organisation. The charter organiser was Seafarer Holidays and the boats were supplied by Aegean Yachts. Both the boats and the flotilla crew were first class. The model works but can and did produce difficulties. Anon.

The itinerary of this flotilla was split between the Gulf of Volos and the Sporades Islands which enabled some crews to choose to take just a one-week flotilla. Not having visited the Gulf before we were quite interested in exploring new territory. However, this hugely increased the overall distance and while the Gulf offers some distractions, it is also a busy commercial and military waterway.

After landing at Skiathos, we were taken by ferry to the base at Loutraki on Skopelos Island. The following morning, after briefings and a short sail, we were swinging to an anchor in Koukounaries Bay on the SW corner of Skiathos. This was something we had done some 30 years earlier, but at that time we did not have to share the bay with acres of beach umbrellas and sunbeds, doughnut rides and pedalos neither were we flown over by parascenders and deafened by multiple beach bars blasting out loud music. Alas, how the Sporades had changed! None the less we enjoyed a nice meal ashore with the lead boat dinghy acting as a taxi.

Then it was post haste to make passage to the Volos Gulf. A conspicuous feature on the coast is a large quarry which serves as a way mark and also as a point of interest in respect of its size. Just before the quarry is a large bay, Khondhri Ammos, which has a secluded cove on the north side. We took lunch here and earmarked it for an overnight stay on our return journey.

So on into the Gulf itself and convenient to the entrance is the village of Palaio Trikeri. It lies in a bay to the north of the channel between Palaio Trikeri Island and the Trikeri Peninsula and affords good shelter from northern meltemi winds. It is not an ideal place for a small yacht since the height of the quay to the south is too high to climb ashore and dictates a dinghy trip to a nearby pontoon. Also, there is a large and conspicuous green water tank which does not enhance the ambiance. However, it is good base to explore the features of the Gulf which lie to the east and the north which we embarked upon the following day.

Ormos Vathoudhi which is protected from the north by Alatis Island is a picturesque and secure bay. Sunsail at one time had a base here on the mainland shore. Our time here was limited since Volos itself at the head of the Gulf was our next destination and involved a passage of 20nm which seemed to take for ever in our small yacht.

Entering Volos Harbour presents an interesting approach. At first sight the entrance is disguised since a groyne to port appears to meet a harbour wall to starboard. Only on closing the Port does it become evident that the two merely overlap leaving a comfortable gap both to pass between the two and to leave the harbour wall to starboard. It is a stimulating place to enter with a constant stream of vessels of all sizes, some very large when seen from the deck of a small yacht, entering and leaving. Eventually, you make your way to the north east corner of Volos Harbour where an old fishing harbour has been turned into a crowded marina. It was nice to be complemented by the lead crew for an inch perfect stern docking in the small space available.

The location is ideal since you step ashore in a city ambience of shops, restaurants and other tourist distractions. A must is to take a taxi up to Makrinitsa on the slopes of Mount Pelion, a treasure trove of historic churches and buildings, restaurants and souvenir shops and to cap it all amazing views of the Gulf. We wined and dined the evening away in a truly wonderful ambience. If you have made it good in Volos, this is where you come to live and many of the older houses have been expensively restored.

At one extremity of our cruising it was now time to embark on a long passage and to retrace our steps back to the Islands. We had a great sail notwithstanding that the passage was in company with commercial and military vessels being overflown by aircraft. We had to be careful that we didn't stray into the military area. With increasing winds, we took shelter in Ormos Nies and relaxed before proceeding to our final stay in the Gulf at Pigadhi. The bay is small, east facing and well sheltered from the north, particularly important in the Meltemi season, and the small projecting quay coped adequately with the arrival of a flotilla. It is a picturesque place with red roofed white cottages gradually ascending the wooded hills behind. It was an ideal rest before the long passage back to Koukounaries.

Our earlier homework served us very well and in an hour or two, we were back at the bay in the northern corner of Khondhri Ammos. It was perfect and we were in no mood to go ashore. We shared the bay with one other boat and this and the shallow depth enabled us to lie to the anchor without taking a line ashore. This is appealing to a geriatric couple since swimming ashore with a fair length of rope presents a challenge as does scrambling to a convenient rock or tree and then hauling the stern round in line. Valerie was once asked by a helpful lady on the beach, 'Why you do this difficult thing?' We always carry a length of light line which can readily be swum ashore and then used to haul in the mooring line. Such a line can also be attached to the tripping ring in rocky anchorages. It takes a moment or two to set and compared to abandoning a lot of chain and an anchor with its flukes lying under a rocky ledge, it makes a lot of sense. Our bottom here was sand with good holding.

Then on to Koukounaries. The wind was from the south so we made a good passage; alas our anchorage at Koukounaries was disturbed by the swell and an unusually cool evening. We looked forward to our next port of call the following day which was Nea Klima on the western side of Skopelos. The harbour surprises since the stone quay which stretches beyond the shallow inner harbour appears at first sight to be somewhat exposed. However, it is well sheltered from the northern Meltemi. It is also a picturesque place to wander around bedecked with colourful bougainvillea bushes. To eat out in a sailing fellowship under a typical red roof in a place like this doesn't get much better.

The next day our activities were determined for us by the lead crew. The message was to get ourselves in to Skopelos Harbour as quickly as we could; a

Meltemi was on its way. We were about to learn aspects of seamanship we had never met before. The conditions on our passage to Skopelos were bumpy but gave no indication as to what was to follow. By late afternoon we were stern to a wide windward quay, lying to two stern lines and an anchor laid out forward almost to full scope. The Meltemi hit us late evening. During the night, the lead boat measured two gusts at severe gale 9 and one at storm force 10. We spent the night in the cockpit. At every gust, the boat surged forward turning the stern lines into elastic bands. Between the gusts we had to power the boat ahead to prevent it being thrown back on to the quay. Mercifully, the lead boat skipper appeared through the rain with a large fender which would not have looked out of place on the QE2.

Drama ensued the following morning with a large ferry appearing at the mouth of the harbour. We do not know whether the Master had permission to enter the harbour or whether he took the responsibility; the outcome is that to get through the swell he entered the harbour at a rate of knots and proceeded on a course which left the moored boats to starboard at the mercy of his wake. The boats nearest to the entry began to rock from side to side and in doing so, aerials and cross trees were carried away. Fortunately, we were sufficiently up the harbour to avoid damage. We had a visit later in the day from what we took to be a Port Official asking if we had heard the ferry sounding any signals; it appeared an investigation into the incident was underway. We were in Skopelos for a further two nights, in part to rest and allow the sea to settle and in part to enjoy its architecture and its hospitality.

With the sea still a bit lumpy we set off for our next destination, Steni Vala on the east coast of Alonnisos. En route we stood into the most easterly of the coves at Ormos Milia. This was a delightful spot with a few white cottages peeping out from wooded hillsides and with low white cliffs and sand fringing the beach which also boasted a restaurant. We were not enticed ashore and were, after our Meltemi, quite pleased to enjoy eating and relaxing on board before continuing to Steni Vala.

The Pilots guide to Steni Vala is to lie bows-to to avoid rudder damage as depths close to shore are down to 1m. The flotilla avoided this by lying to bow anchors well off shore and bringing stern lines ashore. This produced the carnival of crews taking to dinghies from their sterns and having to duck under everyone else's stern line to get to the odd bits of beach. In our case, the nearest bit of beach not yet occupied by several dinghies, was some distance away and involved a scramble to get ashore. However, after the rigours of the Meltemi, we were all up to celebrate our daring-do in the restaurant ashore and a good night was enjoyed.

We woke the following morning with our intentions clear, we would return to Ormos Milia but this time stay overnight. However, before going south we sailed across to Peristeri Island and anchored briefly in Vasiliko Bay. This was again a nostalgia visit to where we had spent free sailing time on our previous flotilla. On that visit here, a flotilla boat had its anchor caught under a chain. We traced the chain back to the shore, put a bight of rope under it, towed the bight to the stern of the trapped boat, lifted the bight and joy of joys the anchor was free. We found Ormos Milia much busier than the day before and, in order to swing if we needed to, we found ourselves in some 8 metres lying to some 20 metres of chain and enjoyed a peaceful night.

We took the anchor up the next morning obeying our usual code: *the anchor should never "pull" the boat, the winch must never be starved of revs and the anchor trip overload must be on*. However, just as we had all the chain up, the winch gave up the ghost. Why, and without a surveyor's report, we will never know. Reporting back to base we were requested to return as quickly as possible so it could be turned around for the next charter. We had sail and engine to enjoy our last day though without an anchor our plans were somewhat thwarted.

However, we couldn't resist briefly revisiting Panormou Bay. What a disappointment; this had been an isolated and dramatic seascape where you could lie to a hook and watch the sun go down in the west. Now it is busy with commerce in the form of tavernas and swimming areas dominating the shores of the main bay and the inset south bay crowded with craft. We also learned a lesson; our emotions intruded into our seamanship and we went very close to the northwest corner of the inset bay, fortunately, we found 3m close too.

Now it was time to return to base. Returning early, we spent time relaxing on the beach at Loutraki while the shore crew ripped our cabin apart looking for an electrical fault. A row ensued as to who was to pay for the damaged windlass, which we felt was heavily overchained. It was eventually resolved by our paying just the damage waiver premium, an opportunity earlier denied to us as we did not want to take out the bundled travel insurance – we had our own, which meant we were no worse off than we expected to be. Also, both parties ended up offering us discounts on a future holiday. We felt a little aggrieved since our anchoring procedure, 'No towing the boat on retrieving the anchor and plenty of neutral revs when the winch is being operated', has stood us in good stead over the years. If a winch is being overloaded to the extent that it "burns out", where was the trip switch?

We had a great flotilla meal and fellowship ahead of the morning ferry back to Skiathos. We shared our cabin overnight with luggage, boxes of leftover food and cabin lining panels stripped off to expose windlass wiring. It didn't matter; we had been challenged in our late seventies and had not been found wanting, buoyed up by the discipline and sense of adventure that sailing brings. In a sense, we had sailed it our way.

Nevertheless, we came home with some feelings of disappointment. The arrival of the Meltemi with the enforced extra stay in Skopelos and the windlass incident denied us the opportunity to visit new destinations north of Steni Vala and to revisit Votsi, Patitiri and the hilltop town of old Alonnisos. As we should have expected, the Sporades Islands had changed and had lost some of the charm that we remembered.

Contrasts of Koukounaries Beach 1984 and 2016

Gulf of Volos from Makrinitsa

Skopelos Harbour before and after the storm

Bareboat

Bareboat Charter 1
Whitsunday Islands, Australia, 1990

This was the main feature of a 3-week break which we managed to arrange in October 1990. Based on the philosophy of making every journey count both in terms of miles and in terms of time, the visit to the Whitsunday Islands got sandwiched between stopovers in Singapore on the way out and Bangkok on the way back.

It is easy to say we flew into Cairns. It's a long way from anywhere when you consider it is further from Perth to Cairns than it is from Singapore to Perth.

While in Cairns, and ahead of flying on to the Whitsundays, we were able to take a Quicksilver catamaran trip out to the Barrier Reef where wonderful facilities including bathing platforms and glass bottomed boats were provided. Being able to explore the undersea world with exotic tropical fish and colourful coral was a real highlight. We also took the Kuranda Scenic Railway trip (World Heritage Listed) through tropical rainforest and spectacular gorges. In the Aboriginal Settlement of Kuranda we were entertained with a traditional show where we watched with fascination the animal like movements and dances. We had one aborigine not only playing a didgeridoo but also a length of Marley drainpipe from which the same sound emanated. Further, my nephew Nigel, who had not long emigrated to Sydney, my sister and brother in law all happened to be in Cairns. We were able to have dinner together; what a coincidence to be the other side of the world at the same time.

Our next destination was the Whitsunday Islands, flying first to Hamilton Island, then back by ferry to Shute Harbour on the mainland where we were to begin our charter. We were enthusiastically received by Australian Bare Boat Charterers with the news of our upgrade to a Farr 38 (Gulp!). This thing had 8 berths, a huge wheel, a gas barbecue in the cockpit, two fridges fully provisioned and a mast that went up for ever. It was the Farr, named "Farr Dinkum", or nothing so with some trepidation off we set. However, the larger yacht did have one particular benefit in enabling us to explore parts of the Islands where navigation is not permitted to craft with a length below 10m.

If you are going to sail in the Whitsundays, an absolute mandate is to have a copy of "100 Magic Miles of the Great Barrier Reef – The Whitsunday Islands" written by David Colfelt and published by Windward Publications Pty. Ltd. The level of pilotage detail given makes navigating these waters very straightforward.

Leaving Shute Harbour, we travelled north off the west coast of Molle Island. Nervously we sailed through "Unsafe Pass" (the pilot was marked 'safe enough for yachts') between North and South Molle Islands, then turned to the east into Cid Harbour, Whitsunday Island, anchoring in Dugong Inlet. This was the start of warm balmy evenings, deserted anchorages, an on-board barbecue (there were singed eyebrows the first night we lit it!) and "ozzie" red to wash it down. Heaven!

The following day we had a long passage, travelling north again. We paused in Nara Inlet and went ashore to inspect some aboriginal cave paintings. We then continued up the west coast of Hook Island and round into beautiful Butterfly Bay. We didn't think a detour into the Hayman Island Resort, a one-time haunt of Princess Margaret, would quite be our scene. Butterfly Bay provided another opportunity to wonder at the colour and shapes of the coral reef. Returning in the dinghy to our boat we were hailed by another yacht anchored in the Bay. The occupants were busy cutting up the results of a fishing trip, a large marlin, and they kindly offered us a couple of steaks. In conversation they asked how long we were sailing. 'Just one week,' we replied. 'And you?'

'Forever,' was their reply.

The next day we retraced our steps and anchored in Stonehaven Bay in some 10m of water. We understood anchoring here can present problems if there are a number of boats, but again we had the place to ourselves. We watched with interest a yellow "submarine" taking visitors from the Hayman Island resort around Black Island reef.

Here we had a rush of blood to the head. We radioed for a seaplane to pick us up from the boat and take us out to the Barrier Reef. The opportunity to make a second visit to the Reef after our Quicksilver experience was too good to miss. The plane landed and anchored downwind from our stern. As instructed, we freed off our dinghy on a long scope and drifted down to the plane and climbed aboard. We were off flying over the reef then able to land close to our very own bit of coral in our own bit of the South Pacific. Magic! As there is quite a tidal range, parts of the reef were exposed and we were able to "reef walk". Recovery was the reverse, the plane "taxiing" up to the dinghy and with the engine stopped, we transferred to the dinghy and shortened the scope taking us back to the Farr's stern.

From here we made a long passage due south down the Whitsunday Passage. We had half a gale on the nose and Valerie was finding it difficult to keep us sufficiently head to wind while I laboured with a massive and heavy sail. We gave it best but had to abandon sailing and motored on passing the west coast of Hook Island and Cid Island before entering the Hunt Channel. We headed towards the Fitzalan Pass, finally taking refuge in Gulnare Inlet. The most striking aspect of this rough passage, in the still warm conditions, was that we were both coated with dried salt. Gulnare Inlet has extensive mangrove creeks which we were able to explore in the dinghy. Here we had a conversation with a crew from a yacht anchored close by who were intrigued with the Welsh flag that we were flying. Once again, the response to 'How long are you sailing?' was 'Forever, we left San Francisco in 1989'.

The following day was to be the antithesis. In pleasant weather, we passed through the Fitzalan Pass north of Hamilton Island, rounded the bottom of Whitsunday Island, turned north through the Solway Passage and emerged with the wonders of Whitehaven Beach to port. We carried on to the northwest and finally rounded Tongue Point and anchored in Tongue Bay. In the morning, we went ashore and climbed to the top of the peninsula and had a magnificent view across to Whitehaven Beach, true to its name with brilliant white sand and turquoise water.

These are the bare facts from the log but they convey nothing of the changing moods and landscapes of the passage culminating in the wild scenario which is Whitehaven Bay. This vista would have been denied us if we hadn't had the upgrade to a 38' boat as navigation through the Solway Passage and the Hook Passage between Hook Island and Whitsunday Island is not permitted for boats < 10 metres in length.

From Tongue Bay, we headed up the east coast of Whitsunday Island to Cateran Bay on the north coast of Border Island. Here we had a mishap. On approaching the bay, our engine temperature alarm sounded and investigation found the face plate of the water-cooling pump had worked loose and its retaining screws were lost in the bilges we knew not where. We had to work very hard putting in a series of tacks in this relatively large boat until we were in the bay and could get a hook down. We radioed ABBC's base and in no time, they had an engineer out to fix it. Now able to continue, we rounded the north coast of Whitsunday Island into Hook Passage, safely passing the two rocks to port. We passed the underwater observatory but did not have time to stop and visit. Then rounding the bottom of Hook Island and, avoiding the shallows, entered Macona Inlet to an anchorage half-way up.

Sadly, it was then our last day. We took a southwest course across the Whitsunday Passage, rounding Molle Island to the east and south and finally took a westerly course to Shute Harbour leaving Shute, Tancred and Repair Islands to port on entry. We had done it and we had a big hug!

After a relaxing stay at the Coral Sea Resort in Airlie Beach, we flew on to Sydney to complete the final stage of our visit to Australia. Here we stayed with friends who have a house on Mosman Creek and a yacht moored off the bottom of the garden. We were taken for a sail around the harbour and witnessed a special Gaffer's Regatta. We were to visit them again in 2017 when the yacht had been replaced by a luxury motor cruiser.

Our time had run out, but our satisfaction cup was overflowing. We had sailed extensively in one of the World's iconic sailing venues and aided, with one exception, with good weather, our seamanship had seen it done. The success of this first distant bareboat charter gave us the confidence to continue to explore other far flung sailing destinations.

Catch of the Day – Marlin

Arrival of the seaplane

Gaffer's Regatta

Sydney Harbour Bridge

Bareboat Charter 2
Intracoastal Waterway, Florida, USA, 1996
St Petersburg - Gulf of Mexico

This charter exceeded expectations. A cruise down the Intracoastal Waterway which runs like a canal between the west coast of Florida and a string of Islands (Keys) fronting the Gulf of Mexico does not at first sight promise a sailing adventure. However, the reality is very different. From just south of the attractive city of St Petersburg and having crossed Tampa Bay, you enter the waterway which wends its way south offering a number of diversions and also the opportunity, at several places, to leave the waterway into the Gulf of Mexico and also to return. The area is seriously attractive and the weather pleasant being warm but at times very humid.

The city of St Petersburg has modern predominantly white buildings which include the Harbourage Marina where "Moorings" had a base, from where we started our cruise. We chartered a Beneteau 352, which had the delightful name "Sunday Morning".

There is an immediate point of interest since to proceed south across Tampa Bay and into the Intracoastal Waterway you have to pass under the Skyway Bridge, an impressive structure where the deck is carried on widely spaced vertical supports. We progressed as far as De Soto Point at the mouth of the Manatee River and anchored. We went ashore to the park and were curious about splashes caused by "divers" in the water offshore; these "divers" turned out to be pelicans fishing. We witnessed a beautiful sunset and later watched impressive flashes of a lightning storm out at sea. We were also fortunate enough to see a manatee, a rare marine mammal commonly known as a sea cow.

The following morning, we sailed into the Intracoastal Waterway and then motored south to Longboat Key. Pleased with our progress and enjoying our cruise, we celebrated with an evening BBQ on the stern of the boat. Well rested, we were now anxious to go to sea so we exited the waterway through the Longboat Pass and sailed in the Gulf down to Venice. We moored at the Crow's Nest Marina where we ate; it was a fascinating place with pelicans in the trees and perched on the vertical wooden jetty poles. Their fishing was even more fun. The Marina gave us a gift in the form of a little box of screwdrivers with the box embossed with their name; I still have it today. As at sea, it is the little things that matter.

The next day we had a long passage down the waterway to Cabbage Key just south of the access to the sea from Charlotte Harbour. Cabbage Key is only accessible by boat. We dined in the Oak House restaurant where a tradition, started over sixty years ago, is for every guest to pin up a signed dollar note somewhere in the restaurant; there must be thousands of dollars up there – we added to the collection.

It was now time to retrace our steps to the north. We sailed up the coast outside the waterway from Boca Grande and re-entered at Venice. We entered a small rectangular cut just south of the entrance but misjudged the depth and grounded in cloying mud. We laid a stern anchor in an attempt to pull us off but to no avail. It was at this time that the local bush telegraph kicked in; motoring proudly into the bay was a large motor craft bearing the legend "Tug Boat Services". Very soon after we were afloat in deeper water but had to dig deep into our pockets. We anchored safely before nightfall.

The next day, we made further progress north using the waterway passing elegant waterside properties; the sin of envy was apparent. Ahead of a bridge, we had to call the bridge master to request passage. The bridge opened for us and we paid the bill in a net on the end of a pole proffered to us; the nicest thing was that the bridge master said, 'Thank you, CAPTAIN.'

Following an overnight stay in the harbour at Sarasota City, we set off across Sarasota Bay. However, we were quickly overtaken by a rainstorm which reduced the visibility and produced fluky winds. We had set out with the simple view that if the bow is pointing directly at a visible destination and there are no shallows between us and that destination, all we had to do was to follow the line of sight to the destination. This was courting disaster. Wind and tide were displacing us from our original compass course and taking us over shallows indicated by loud bleeps from the echo sounder. Our safe course had to be along a line between our destination and an agreed fixed point on land behind us. We were steering line of sight only to a visible objective and it was only when we woke up to the fact that wind and tide were changing our bearing that we realised our predicament. Good seamanship is constant vigilance. The visibility was so poor that we had a job to discern the channel markers and were much relieved to exit the Bay and return to the narrower confines of the Waterway.

Anchoring again at Longboat Key, we went ashore and walked across to the beach where we swam. Also on the beach we saw many turtle nests roped off to prevent interference during the breeding season.

Then it was time to return to St Petersburg which has a cultural appeal. The Sears family, who introduced catalogue shopping into the USA, collected a large number of Salvador Dali pictures including "Columbus arriving in America" and others showing his interest in crystallography. They offered the collection to any city which would provide a Gallery to show them; St Petersburg was selected. Our last and very pleasant diversion was a visit to the Salvador Dali Gallery where we bought a folio of Dali's pictures.

Leaving aside that there was not a lot of sailing at sea and that we were often motoring in the Waterway, this charter gave constant diversion in a variety of ways. Do not be dissuaded by the view that this is more of a "canal" holiday than cruising under sail.

We had come to Florida primarily to sail. However, we pursued our philosophy of making every journey count and hired a car and drove to Orlando. Here we did the Disney things, Seaworld and Epcot and made a trip across to Cape Kennedy to visit the space station. Returning to Tampa, our arrival airport, we flew on to New Orleans. Staying in the French Quarter we were well placed to enjoy the jazz scene, in particular at Preservation Hall. Other tourist attractions were to take a tram ride around the historic part of the city and a Mississippi boat trip to the Battlefields and back on the paddle steamer "Natchez". This was floating of a different kind!

Cabbage Key, Florida

Paddle Steamer "Natchez", New Orleans

Bareboat Charter 3
Bay of Islands, New Zealand, 2001

We were fortunate on our trip to New Zealand's Bay of Islands. Our niece's father-in-law retired to New Zealand and set up a hotel business in Paihia run by our niece and her husband which enabled them also to settle in New Zealand. Hence we had "aides de camp" in place on our arrival a short distance from Opua where we were to start our charter from the Moorings Charter Company. We spent a couple of days ashore before embarking during which we were able to take in some local landmarks and history.

Paihia is close to Waitangi where the treaty which bears its name was signed by Maori Chiefs ceding New Zealand to Queen Victoria's empire. The site and the area is full of history from the ornately decorated ceremonial barge to the Treaty House and grounds. Nearby is Motuarohia Island, which we were to visit during our charter, where Captain Cook landed over 200 years ago and Keri Keri which was one of New Zealand's first trading posts. We also had the opportunity to do a forest walk behind Paihia which was our first introduction to the rich flora, fauna and falls found everywhere in New Zealand.

Then we were off to the waterfront at nearby Opua to pick up a Hunter 320 called "Karoro" which was to be our home for the next 8 days. She was well appointed and well balanced and a joy to sail even in boisterous conditions. We particularly liked the twin transom seats mounted high up on the after-cockpit rails. We left Opua mid-afternoon and after an hour or two of running and gybing we anchored in Pomare Bay, a large bay with a number of coves around its edges, where we enjoyed a pleasant evening with all anchor bearings constant. The forecast was for winds of 15 knots from the south which we knew from research could give us a metre or so of swell out at Cape Brett.

The following day we were again favoured with runs and reaches, with boat speed up to 5.6 knots, except while motoring upwind. We had a run out of

Pomare Bay, gybed off Waitangi under the bows of the anchored cruise liner "Regal Princess" on to a northerly course to run up to the headland at Fraser Rock. From here we had a beam reach to Cliff Rock from which we motored south against the wind between Motukiekie Island and Urupukapuka Island; the island names give you a sense of sailing in Maori waters. We anchored in the aptly named Paradise Bay, which we had to ourselves, and were immediately tempted to a run ashore. There is a delightful walk along the beach to the next bay, Otaio Bay. With the forecast for the next day promising SE winds at 20 knots and 1 metre swell, we re-anchored in the south part of the bay to give us a little more shelter. Our evening was genuinely moving, here we were, two souls entwined by some unfathomable destiny sitting in a fibre glass box the other side of the world. We sang: "Who can explain it, who can tell you why?"

Dawn the next day was decision time. We were heading out to the mouth of the Bay of Islands. The overnight forecast gave us SE at 20 knots. If we were going to Whangaroa we would be faced with a bumpy passage past the Cavalli Islands, concluding with trying to find an entrance on a lee shore rock face which is difficult to discern. Further and more daunting was the prospect of exiting into and returning against a pattern of wind stuck at 20 knots. A brief discussion concluded that we were not here to prove anything to anyone and that staying in the Bay was both a sensible idea and sensible seamanship.

Hence we found ourselves running north with Okahu Island to starboard and gybing round the rocks atop of the island, with no sign of Whale Rock to port, on a course to Cape Brett. There was a big swell off the Cape which we passed white knuckled and close hauled in each direction with a tack between them and stemming crests up 2 metres off the Hole in the Rock. Meanwhile a tourist boat with I don't know how many horsepower was making passage through the "Hole". Then with some relief we opted for a broad reach back towards Motutara Rock which we left to starboard. We then settled onto starboard tack, with one reef and a boat speed of 7 knots, down to Oke Bay where we anchored. It has a crescent shaped beach with beautiful white sand and several trails, one of which gives some spectacular views of Cape Brett. It was well worth the run ashore. Later we were hardly conscious of the drizzle, only conscious that the stern gland was leaking and needed the nut tweaked to keep the automatic bilge pump quiet. Sigh; just another day's sailing but we'd made it!

The morning brought a further forecast of 20 knot winds so we felt we had made the right decision the day before; we still had some difficult navigation ahead of us. A good start allowed us a beam reach through the Albert Channel from the north, leaving Hat Island to starboard and Tu Hue to port. On this passage we were accompanied by a pod of dolphins playing under our bows. The next way point was the Paramena Beacon from where we had a dead run up to Motuarohia Island, also called Roberton Island, which demands a visit due both to its charm and history.

It is a delightful place with two bays, Cooks Cove and Twin Lagoon Bay. Cooks Cove is so named since it was here that Captain Cook visited the Bay of Islands in 1769. Twin Lagoon Bay is so called since the topography of the shore ensures that two "lagoons" of water are retained as the tide recedes. In northerly gales, water surges into the lagoons from the other side of the island and almost splits the island into three. There is a trail which takes you to the highest point; there are a lot of steps but the effort is worth it for the wonderful view looking down on the south shore. The combination of bays, lagoons and walks makes it a popular lunchtime stay. The alternative name, Roberton Island, arises from the time the island was privately owned; a farmer called Bull was murdered here in a dispute with local Maories. Our day ended with a longish upwind passage under engine back to the shelter of Omakiwi Cove being careful to miss Shag Rock at its entrance. This is an attractive anchorage in southerly winds.

The next day dawned with the wind now more easterly than southerly. We decided to go dolphin hunting back up toward the Albert Channel where we had seen them previously. We were still able to sail close hauled up between Te Ao and Mahenotiti Islands south of the Albert Channel, but alas no dolphins. We went as far as the conical buoy at the north end of Urupukapuka Island and then retraced our steps to Cable Bay protected behind Round Island. This wasn't tenable with the wind in the east and so, rounding Poroporo Island, we headed north to Otaio Bay but in the end preferred to retrace our steps into the familiar Paradise Bay for a lunch stop. Later we reached from Paradise Bay to Motukauri Island at the end of the spit which encloses Manawaora Bay, tacked into the Bay and anchored in Opunga Cove, a convenient place from which to take our niece and her husband for a sail the following day.

We motored across to Paihia next morning and while Valerie stood off, I went by dinghy to collect our niece Judith and her husband Paul who were waiting on the beach in Te Ti bay. All aboard we set off and had a splendid beam reach with Paul at the helm and Judith getting a dousing with lee rail almost under! We again encountered a pod of dolphins but they did not approach the yacht as closely as before. We went north of Moturua Island and then turned SE through the channel between Moturua Island and Motukiekie Island and anchored in Awaawaroa Bay for lunch. This Bay is more commonly known as Pipi Bay and sometimes as Honeymoon Bay. Our return passage was more gentle with a following wind. The young people had had a great day of relaxation and we deposited them back on the beach for them to resume the running of the Swiss Chalet Lodge Motel.

We ended our day anchored in Kororareka Bay, the main anchorage for Russell, and went ashore. It is a historical and picturesque village with a number of cafes and restaurants along the waterfront; we paused at the colonial styled Duke of Marlborough Hotel for a drink. Further along is the old police station, built in 1870, which served as the custom house until 1890. Since then it has served as the police station and residence. Alongside is a huge Morton Bay Fig tree planted by the first customs officer. Behind the main street is located the small office of the guy who each morning broadcasts the weather/shipping forecast for the Bay of Islands; we called in and thanked him for his service. Following a trail north of the town we climbed up to Flagstaff Hill. The Union Jack was first hoisted here in 1840 but in subsequent disputes the flagstaff was chopped down four times. The views from here are stunning with a 360-degree vista of the Bay of Islands.

Sadly, the following morning it was time to return to base at Opua. We had had a great week's sailing in an iconic place but our exploration of New Zealand had only just begun. We went on to visit other highlights of the country including Auckland, the hot springs at Rotorua, the vineyards near Napier and the city of Wellington on North Island. Then crossing to South Island, we donned crampons for a walk on Franz Josef glacier, took a helicopter flight landing on Mount Cook, punted on the canal in Christchurch's Botanical Gardens and took a boat trip on Milford Sound plus many more special experiences. This was truly a special holiday.

Roberton Island (Cook Cove)

Approaching "The Hole in the Rock"

Punting in Christchurch

Bareboat Charter 4
Langkawi, Malaysia, 2002

One of our guiding principles in life has always been to make every journey count. At the beginning of the new century, the opportunity to travel world-wide was taking off and we were anxious to be part of it. In particular, China was opening up and we were fortunate to find a tour which gave us access to many of China's attractions including a walk along the Great Wall. We were also on the last ferry boat to go up the Yangtze River before they closed it to complete the dam – trucks began to deposit boulders into the river astern of us as we passed through. Further up river there were signs high up on the enclosing hills which indicated the depth to prevail upstream of the dam.

Having spoiled ourselves in China and spent time with friends in Hong Kong we couldn't resist exploring the sailing opportunities in the Far East. So we arranged a charter out of Kuah on the Island of Langkawi.

Langkawi comprises a group of Islands (an Island is a "pulau") of which Langkawi is the largest. The other main islands are Langgun and Timun to the east and Singa Besar and Dayang Bunting to the south. Langkawi has high ground rising from the shore in the northwest; in the northeast the high ground has cliffs above the coast. Elsewhere at sea level the waterfront is a sandy beach backed by verdant rainforest.

After an overnight stay at the Sheraton luxury resort (now the Westin Resort), we made our way to the Sunsail Base located at the Royal Langkawi Yacht Club and after the usual formalities we set sail in an Oceanis 33 towards Pulau Dayang.

Once under way, we headed south to a beautiful and deserted bay on the east side of Pulau Tuba. The southern bays on Langkawi are very similar comprising prolific green trees and bushes running down to sandy beaches "ironed" flat by the gentle lapping of calm seas. Unfortunately, our domestic battery went down and we were forced to return to the Yacht Club the following morning for a replacement. We spent most of the day enjoying the facilities at the Royal Langkawi Yacht Club. Battery repaired we set sail and resumed our passage along the coast of Pulau Dayang Bunting, again anchoring in a bay on Pulau Tuba.

Next day, at the extreme southwest corner of Dayang Bunting we found a delightful bay to anchor. We took the dinghy to a narrow jetty and from here a 10-minute walk through the forest led us to the Lake of the Pregnant Maiden which was attractive if a little oddly named. It is a large lake surrounded by hills having dense rain forest and although only 30 metres of rock separate it from the sea the lake is freshwater. The legend of the lake is that a Princess having laid her dead baby son to rest in the lake then blessed all women having difficulty in conceiving a child. They would become fertile once having taken a dip in the water of the lake. Though unproven it remains a strong belief among locals. There were swimming pontoons on the edge of the lake and the venue was popular with visitors.

We proceeded further south into the Malaccan Straight, a connection between the Bay of Bengal and the South China Sea. We had a sense of being between the Indian Ocean and the North Pacific Ocean.

The quality of Langkawi's beaches cannot be understated plus the fact that years ago you could have a whole beach to yourself shared only with monkeys swinging in the trees. The next place we found was one such with Valerie emerging from the shallows in her costume as sole occupier. It became our Ursula Andress moment likened to that from the James Bond classic "Dr No".

Our circumnavigation of Pulau Dayang was now complete and we headed for the south west corner Langkawi Island itself. Our first port of call was Telaga Harbour. This was a quite extraordinary place to visit. Remember, this is 2002 before modern marina developments and what we found was an eclectic mix of buildings and boats spread out on each side of the creek. Even more amazing was the fellowship of the crews that occupied the boats. Many of these were awaiting the return of the owners who had left to earn money to meet the "lien notices" (boat being held in lieu of debts) pinned to their masts. Others just seemed to have "lost bottle" for the big sailing adventure. There was an organised social programme listed on a notice board together with notices like "will swap fan belt for head sail". Make sure your next great adventure is financially secure!

Telaga offers some shelter from hurricanes but is not as secure a bolt hole as one in the north coast which we visited later.

We moved on towards the west coast of Langkawi making passage to Berjaya Langkawi Beach Resort with its red roofed chalets perched on stilts above the water. A relaxing few hours were spent here using the pool and facilities. Then rounding the northwest corner, we anchored in Datai Bay and went ashore to the Andaman Hotel Resort.

From here we were able to take a taxi to the Skyline Cable Car which had recently opened. From the top there were spectacular views across all the islands. In recent years this facility now has a Skyline bridge, a lightweight girder structure which enhances the experience. We returned to the Andaman Hotel for dinner.

Next day, we had an invigorating sail along the north coast of Langkawi to the northeast corner. This differs from the more southerly areas in as much as it comprises steep cliffs along the way rather than the more picturesque bays to the south. Some of these cliffs appear to have been eroded at their base to the extent that one can almost navigate with a rock projection above your head. The effect is quite dramatic. At other points, the landscape has been penetrated by narrow gorges of water with bays and channels branching off them. We went on between Pulau Langgun and the main island to the "Hole in the Wall", or the sailor's hideaway. This is tucked between towering cliffs and is part of the Kilim Karsh Geopark and serves as a boat park where owners can safely leave their boats during the hurricane season. We explored the retreat by dinghy passing mangroves lining the creeks.

Then all too soon we were on passage back to the charter base. We had a little time to explore Kuah, the main town, by foot before taking our flight home via Kuala Lumpur. Future voyagers will find Langkawi changed; the idyllic coast line is beginning to see resorts and diversions which, enjoyable in their own right, will steal away the feeling of being in a wild and natural place.

Lake of the Pregnant Maiden   Overhanging Cliffs

"Hole in the Wall", Kilim Karsh Geopark

Bareboat Charter 5
The Seychelles, 2003

Our voyaging up to this point had developed quite an international flavour and this begged the question where else in the world could we go. It also begged the question where could we go to escape the onset of winter at home which invites a focus on the southern hemisphere. So was born the Seychelles project. The project was also attractive to Janet and David Dick and to Bill and Kay Abbott with whom we had sailed together in the British Virgin Islands 3 years previously. Further, a visit to the Seychelles in their early spring would avoid the arrival of late strong south easterly winds consistent with the anticyclonic conditions met in the southern hemisphere.

So in November we found ourselves on the quay at Victoria, the capital city on the island of Mahe, the largest of the Seychelles Islands. We went with Sunsail who had just taken over a local company and Sunsail's standards had not had a chance to prevail. Our boat, a Jeanneau 42 called "Oeil de Tigre", was not as tidy as we would have liked with a loose floorboard in the cabin sole, which was fixed, and one of the two heads not functioning which they didn't fix. Briefing began as you arrived; then as the next crew arrived briefing started all over again! Having said that, the support received during difficulties encountered on the charter was exemplary. The ladies set off by taxi to get provisions from a supermarket which was a waste of time as the shelves were virtually empty. Apparently, there was a much better supermarket but we were in the hands of the taxi driver. After a somewhat fraught start, we dined at the Pirates Club and began to relax and feel more at home.

We set sail the next day to make passage to Praslin Island leaving the Isle St Anne to port. After a late start and with 20 miles to cover, we opted to motor sail and by midday we were anchored off the Saint Pierre Islet. Don't mock motor sailing. It is often the best way to enjoy a voyage with the wind in your sails but is often a smoother and faster way to proceed. The snorkelling was great providing close up views of brightly coloured shoals of fish and a turtle.

When we tried to leave, our anchor was trapped in coral. We asked for help from Sunsail and they responded promptly. Their seamanship was pragmatic. If your gypsy is worn so that it slips, rather than lift chain vertically at the bow, just place an unshod foot on the chain as it rises over the gypsy; the chain snags nicely in the gypsy! (Don't try this for yourselves!).

St Pierre Islet lies off the Anse Volbert, a 3k long very pleasant beach with a number of restaurants. We anchored off the beach; our outboard was reluctant to start so we rowed ashore and enjoyed a creole meal.

The following day dawned with the same idyllic weather and we made passage to Isle Curieuse, a wilderness bursting with interest. Every shade of green was discernible in its flora and fauna and we were confronted with bright red birds, Madagascar Fodys, and 90-year-old giant tortoises. We had an enjoyable walk which took in a redundant turtle breeding pond and also what we thought was a whale but turned out to be Bill who had gone for a swim; we all joined him on the beautiful beach! The day ended celebrating Bill's birthday at the "La Reserve" hotel with its beautiful restaurant built out on stilts above the water at Anse Volbert.

Provisioning was now on the agenda and this was achieved by motor sailing round Praslin to the quay at Baie St Anne where we took a taxi to the local supermarket; Kay also purchased some local fish. Then it was off to explore the Cocos Islands; snorkelling here was quite challenging due to a strong current but we were rewarded with more turtle activity. On our return, we looked at staying at La Digue but found the small harbour full and were concerned that the bays to the south would be exposed if the wind strengthened. We carried on back to Anse Volbert and enjoyed a beautiful sunset and a fry up on board.

The next day we had set aside for a visit to Aride since local literature indicated we could land on a Friday. We had a boisterous sail to the south east coast where we anchored and called ashore by phone and radio. Disappointingly, there was no response and we were nervous about going ashore both for protocol and weather reasons. Eventually we gave up and motored to the elevated west corner of the island where we could see frigate birds soaring. A few blasts on the fog-horn markedly increased this activity and it was quite a spectacle. However, there were no other options but to return to the convenient location of Baie St Anne where we anchored.

On Saturday, to ensure access to the harbour, we caught the ferry across to explore the island of La Digue. On arrival we were delighted to discover we could do this on bicycles. So equipped, we were off to find stunning beaches, large polished rocks fashioned by the elements, ox-carts, big tortoises, and coconuts all of which gave the impression of being in an exceptional place. We returned to Baie St Anne feeling we had had a special day.

At Baie St Anne we were seduced by a quiet ambience into anchoring on a short scope between rows of boats on permanent moorings tucked between the pier and a close, walled shoreline. To this day, our conscience is still troubled by this lapse. Suffice it to say that overnight we had a northerly squall which had we been abed would have pushed us against the shoreline wall. As it was, we had the engine on in time to avoid this but we now needed to get the hook up. Precious seconds were lost locating the anchor trip switch in the dark during which our yawing about was endangering local craft. Fortunately, our plight had been observed by Sunsail staff who helped us escape the moorings and tie up to the pier. The staff were then off to aid a catamaran which was aground on rocks.

Our berth on the town quay enabled both early provisioning and a visit to the Vallee de Mai where a small forest has grown with tree species unique to the world. In particular the fruit of the Coco de Mer, with its buttock like appearance, can grow to an enormous size – the world record is 17 kilos for a single nut! We were also fortunate to get a sighting of rare black parrots, again unique to this area. After lunch it was back to Anse Volbert to rest and this time our meal ashore was Pizzas at Berjaya's.

Monday provided a perfect beam reach to Grand Soeur (4.8 kts). Snorkelling here was as good as it gets demanding two sessions, before and after lunch. Again, we were able to "dance" with hawksbill turtles and had sightings of a range of tropical fish: reef shark, clownfish, emperor angelfish, to name just a few. Then it was a broad reach back to Anse Volbert where we celebrated fellowship and seamanship with an on-board feast in the moonlight.

Next morning required an early start with a motor sail to Cousin which is a nature reserve and bird sanctuary. Here you are met by tenders to take you ashore to a natural wilderness. We were taken on a guided walk where we observed many tropical birds, including the rare blue pigeon, hermit crabs, and fruit bats and learned about sticky seed trees. You have the chance to "launch" ground nesting long tailed tropic birds into flight. It is a stunning place to visit. Then it was a long, lumpy, passage back towards Mahe; we anchored off Round Island in the St Anne Marine National Park.

On our last day at sea we had a lively sail circumnavigating Isle St Anne accompanied by a pod of dolphins, then anchored off Moyenne Island for snorkelling prior to a fry up of galley remnants. We re-anchored off Round Island and went ashore by dinghy, meeting the Warden on our exploratory walk. Then, reluctantly, it was time to motor, head to wind, back to Mahe with the profound satisfaction of delivering the boat back onto a mooring at the Sunsail base. We were greeted by a terrible smell from the canning factory but were entertained watching the amazing skills in net making. We celebrated our successful voyage at Sam's Pizzeria in Victoria.

Charter periods do not always tie in with, for example, scheduled flights, so that there is often the opportunity to tag on extra days locally ahead of a flight home. In our case this was a taxi ride away in the form of the Beauvallon Bay Hotel; with its beach side location it was a wonderful place to relax after the challenges of our charter. We also took separate excursions, David, Valerie and Neil to swim at the Port Launay National Park, while Bill, Kay and Janet hired a car to visit schools and museums reflecting local life. A further day of relaxing on the beach with walks along the sands and swimming in warm turquoise waters made a perfect ending to our holiday.

The flight home took a course right up the middle of the Red Sea giving spectacular views including those of the pyramids outside Cairo.

Valerie "sitting" on giant Tortoise

Typical rock forms on beach at La Digue

Coco Du Mer

Bareboat Charter 6
Gulf Islands, Canada, 2004

The decision to go and sail in the Gulf Islands off the coast of Vancouver was born several years earlier. Ever on the lookout for a bargain, we read that Lunn Poly was linking up with Princess Cruises to promote a tour in British Columbia. The tour was by road around Banff Springs and Lake Louise followed by a cruise from Vancouver up the west coast of Alaska to Glacier Bay in the north. What's more, you got to stay and eat at the Banff Springs Hotel and at Chateau Lake Louise. It was almost a bribe to come. Alongside the pleasure of the scenery and watching icebergs calving in Glacier Bay and enjoying the City of Vancouver, we also had tantalising glimpses of the sailing possibilities while on a boat excursion to Victoria on Vancouver Island. These were reinforced later by a business conference visit to Vancouver from which Neil returned by Canadian Pacific to Calgary and from its couchette was able to watch the head of the train "bridging" over its tail.

With many thanks to the Gould family who put us up at their home in West Vancouver the previous evening, we found ourselves in the Bayshore Marina wheeling a supermarket trolley towards a Dufour 36 called "Nonna" chartered from Sunsail. Even in the Bayshore Marina, it was quite a climb from marina pontoon up on to the deck of the boat, something we met throughout the charter. Another factor we were aware of before setting sail is that the water temperature is not conducive to swimming. Then we were off and enjoying the thrill of passing down the First Narrows and under the iconic Lion's Gate Bridge. One navigational hazard we had not encountered before was to avoid the flight path of float planes taking off.

The Vancouver Strait (Georgia Strait is its actual name) can be a rough crossing; to reduce the impact of this, we elected to round Point Atkinson into Howe Sound from where we could make a "dash" if required. We anchored in

Mannion Bay and had a run ashore in delightful Snug Harbour. Our cautions were somewhat misplaced since the following day we had a lively but reasonably comfortable passage, despite the occasional 20kt gust, and made landfall at the Silva Bay Marina on Gabriola Island. Having reached the Gulf Islands, we enjoyed a celebration meal on the roof terrace of the marina watching, amongst other things, seaplanes dropping off their passengers at the marina quay.

The challenge next day was to navigate the Gabriola Pass. Ample warning is given in the Pilot Books that at slack water, you will not be the only craft with a course through the Gabriola Pass. So it proved to be and we had to tuck in very close to the shore to avoid several tug boats towing log rafts which appeared to be acres in size. Once through the pass, the easy option is to head to Wally's Bay at the south end of De Courcy Island which is ahead as you exit the pass. It is snug a little rock fringed inlet with a beach at its head and almost has the feel of a country estate lake as much as a tidal cove. From here you can walk to Pirates Cove which is similar but larger and which has a much narrower and shallow entrance. We had company in the form of small deer peering at us from bushes under the red Arbutus trees set back from the rock fringes and from raccoons who were dashing about almost under our feet. At one time, De Courcy Island was occupied by a sect who believed in the enslavement of women (Neil, 'Damn – missed the boat again!') We ended our day anchoring in Telegraph harbour on the south of Thetis Island. There is a shallow cut here which leads to Clam bay on the other side of Thetis Island which we explored when we returned later in the cruise. The harbour at dawn the next day was like a mill pond.

After each peaceful dawn, it is difficult to move on but move on we must. Continuing going south we passed seals basking off Kuper Island before turning across the top of Saltspring Island en route to Wallace Island with its two bays, Princess Bay and Conover Cove. Conover Cove, named after the man who developed it over many years of hard work and enterprise, became a resort with cottages, wharfs and features for boats. It is now part of the Wallace Island Marine Park. The cove has a number of drawbacks in that it is both small and shallow, difficult to enter and exit and anchoring requires a line ashore. A much easier option, which we took, is to anchor in the adjacent Princess Bay where there is both depth and room to swing. We anchored here and were rewarded with a magnificent sunset. We also had the unusual experience of fending off a large log floating horizontally in the water and moving up tide, only a couple of hours later, having to fend it off as it moved down tide. Elsewhere we met logs floating vertically, a more significant hazard.

Our next port of call the following day was Ganges Harbour Marina on Saltspring Island via the Trincomali Channel. An intriguing aspect of this marina was that it was run by the local Rotary Club. (On my return to my Rotary Club in Cardiff, a motion that we should put in a bid to run Cardiff Bay alas was not carried!). We enjoyed a pleasant dinner at the "Oyster Catcher" and the next day we made an early passage across to Winter Cove on Saturna Island since we had set our hearts on climbing Mount Warburton.

From the Cove it was hard work since we had quite a distance to cover over the level ground before the ground began to rise. The approach to the summit was frustrating and involved a number of artificial horizons as well as steep slopes. However, we eventually emerged from the woodland and were greeted to an amazing view looking out over Saturna Beach across the Gulf Islands. We retraced our steps and feeling very tired when a passing motorist gave us a lift the remainder of the way back to Winter Cove. Once again, we witnessed another incredible sunset. We shared Winter Cove with Bald Eagles, Robins, Vultures and Buzzards and, naturally, Canadian Geese. We also watched a number of boats shooting Boat Pass into Winter Cove; slack water is unpredictable both in time and direction and boat speed is needed to keep anything approaching a straight course.

The following day we resisted the urge to go and explore what looked like seriously rich Boot Cove and made passage round to Saturna Beach. We understood that boatie gatherings are held off the beach but although it is relatively shallow water over sand, we weren't sure of its holding so we didn't go ashore to the beach.

Next stop was at Bedwell harbour on South Pender Island. This area is part of the Beaumont Marine Park which was appealing; in particular we enjoyed a great meal at the Poets Corner Resort in the harbour.

We had a great sail to Sidney Marina with 14 knots of wind and then had a day out at Buchart Gardens. We contemplated sailing round to approach the gardens from Todd Inlet but a short taxi ride appealed more than a long sail. We contented ourselves with a picture of Todd Inlet where otherwise we would have landed. We had visited the Gardens on a previous visit to Vancouver Island but it still impressed with its superb colourful displays.

The time had come to turn to the north and begin to retrace our steps towards Nanaimo from where we planned to re-cross the Strait. However, we had some catching up to do on the way. We had not taken in the gems of Saltspring Island on the way down so we took in the Three Beaches Cove, the Ruckle Provincial Park and the Montague Harbour Provincial Marine Park, Galiano Island, on the way back. Again we were conscious of the large ferries using Active Pass; our "big" boat seemed a lot smaller in their company but still a joy to sail as we retraced out steps to Telegraph Bay. Here we couldn't resist a dinghy trip through the cut to have a look at Clam Bay, a fun diversion. Then continued the serious business of making ground to the north. Following lunch at Herring Bay on the north of Ruxton Island, we weaved an unsteady course through the Dodd Narrows and found our way to a berth in Nanaimo Marina.

Here we had a day or two in hand to make our return passage through the Strait. We made good use of this time. Nanaimo exudes charm and tradition; the noon cannon is fired every day. We also made a visit to Newcastle Island and took dinner at the Dinghy Dock Pub on Protection Island. The fish and chips were to die for; you got the impression the fish had leapt out of the water straight into the pan so fresh was the dish. A highlight was taking a float plane trip with Baxter Air and viewing from above all the areas that we had sailed.

There followed a nervous wait for the morning of our passage to Vancouver. In the end it was comfortable enough and we were only moderately tired but highly satisfied when we splashed out for a berth in the Snug Cove Marina on Bowen Island. Then back under the bridge, a dutiful call at the fuel dock and then a safe return to the Bayshore Marina with no broken gear, skin or bones. There isn't a scale that can measure the satisfaction in two souls in their sixties who came and made a voyage with equal measures of anxiety and anticipation. Our god came with us.

We completed our holiday in Canada by having a few days at Whistler where we took the chair to the top of Whistler Mountain, were nearly tempted to ski on Blackthorn Mountain and were awakened early one morning by a bear trying to raid the bins.

Meeting the Log Tow

Sunset in Princess Bay

Morning Calm Telegraph Harbour

Bareboat Charter 7
French Polynesia, 2005

A long-harboured dream of ours was to sail to Bora-Bora in French Polynesia; a destination not well known in early days. We were able to put together our response with a visit with Janet and David Dick, the couple we had met on an early flotilla holiday when our children were young and with whom we went on to enjoy a number of bare-boat and flotilla holidays in a variety of locations. It was a complicated arrangement since Janet and David's son now lives in San Francisco where Janet and David also have a house. We tied up the journeys by their flying from San Francisco to Los Angeles to meet us off a flight from London. We then flew on together to Tahiti and finally to Raiatea. We were greeted at the Sunsail base with a traditional lei; a garland of fresh flowers. Our charter boat was a Beneteau Oceanis 423 with the rather inauspicious name "Grapefruit".

The initial stages of any charter are challenging. Not only do you have to get used to the boat which requires adequate briefing but you also have to attend to provisioning for the voyage. In this case, it involved a short passage under engine to Baie Tepua. We had been advised to pick up a mooring buoy off the town quay but couldn't find one which gave us sufficient depth; at length we diverted directly to the town quay. Having procured a wealth of provision options, we settled down to a well-earned rest disturbed only by the need to close hatches against some rain.

Next morning, we had some difficulty getting going as there was a strong wind blowing us hard against the quay. Once away we were off under sail to the Island of Tahaa which shares the same lagoon as the Island of Raiatea. We were immediately privileged to witness a great spectacle, being the start of the Hawaiki Nue outrigger canoe race on its stage to Bora-Bora to the northwest. The canoes move quickly and therefore the pursuing spectator boats have to move quickly; the spectator boats covered everything from a large catamaran to small day boats. They follow the race in pursuit finally exiting the coral reef through the Paipai Pass. This was nautical bedlam the like of which none of us had seen before.

We sailed on past this spectacle and anchored off Motu Tautau with its resort of thatched accommodation built on stilts into the bay. This was a splendid place to snorkel, revealing purple coral, multi-coloured fish and huge sea slugs on the sandy bottom. Towards evening, we motored across to the shelter of Tapuamu Bay for a night anchored against a back drop of Mount Teta.

The next day saw us up at 6 am and underway to Bora Bora at 7 am and with a force 5 behind us we ran down under main and engine, giving us a straight and steady course without helm adjustments. It was quite daunting identifying the entrance to the pass through the coral reef with the surf breaking; so with relief we entered the calm waters of the lagoon. We then spent time snorkelling over coral which was like a nursery for small fish; the penalty we paid was having to use the engine and the winch to retrieve the anchor from the coral (see comments in Seychelles Flotilla on running angle of chain over gypsy). After a delightful day, we motor-sailed to the southern end of Bora-Bora's Povai Bay. Here we enjoyed the courtesy of a mooring buoy and a wonderful meal at the renowned "Bloody Mary's" restaurant.

The following day the wind was gusty, to be expected in an area dominated by a high peak. The mountain peak of Bora-Bora, Mt Otemanu, rising above the low-level seascape has to be one of the World's iconic sights and we had a genuine sense of privilege at being here. This did not deter us from making passage under sail to get round to the NE of Bora Bora with the lagoon bordered by the eastern reef. Our draft was 1.9m and the lagoon had depths down to 2m: we steered the boat via hand signals from a crew member standing on the foredeck. Anchoring off Motu Tupe we went ashore to visit the Lagoonarium.

The Lagoonarium was enticing fun. To be sharing the same containment of water with sharks, rays, turtles and catfish and then to chase small fish through tropical coral was just magic. So were the vittles they supplied to us, an abundance of fresh tropical fruit.

The next day with confidence in our procedure with a "human" depth meter on the foredeck, we motored further south to the west of the main coral reef, turning at its end to enter the buoyed channel which enabled us to return safely to the north. We pressed on around the top of the central island to anchor off Bora Bora Yacht Club opposite the Teavanui Pass.

Bora Bora Yacht Club was not particularly friendly initially denying us access to a mooring buoy or a meal ashore. We hung on to the mooring buoy and went ashore; walking into town we did some shopping and booked a table at the "Pirates Bar". After Happy Hour at the Yacht Club and a shower and change on board, we were back at the Club waiting for the lift the "Pirates Bar" said they would arrange. This didn't appear so in the end the yacht club manager gave us a lift. The meal made up for all the hassle.

After a swelly night and a morning's snorkelling off Motu Ahune, we set sail for Huahine. We chose the northern passage. Sadly, we had to motor all the way to the Passe Avamoa and an anchorage off Fare. This offered us a shopping expedition in a pleasant town.

The next day, having watered at the quay, we stayed at anchor while we took a guided tour by car around the island which took in vanilla plantations, maree (burial grounds) and mountain viewpoints. Later in the day we motored down through the marked channel to Avea Bay at Point Tiva. We enjoyed idyllic swimming and snorkelling with lots to see or just lying on white sand under coconut trees. We had dinner ashore at a restaurant where they entertained us with a demonstration of 101 ways to wear a sarong.

After a peaceful night, we woke to cloudy conditions; our best option was a walk along the beach to a second nearby restaurant for coffee followed by snorkelling. Then we took a short sail back along the coast to a very snug anchorage which we shared with two other boats.

All good things must come to an end and it was Saturday and time to start retracing our steps to Raiatea. We left Huahine at 8.30 am and entered the lagoon through the Toahotu Pass to the east of Tahaa. We anchored of a small island just north of the pass. It was here we committed the cardinal sin of casting off the dinghy without ensuring the oars were on board and, of course, the outboard wouldn't start. Fortunately, there was another boat between us and the coral reef so we came to no harm.

Next morning, we motored on south down the east coast of Raiatea hoping to find a snorkelling beach but to no avail. We took lunch and then motored back to base where we were provided with a mooring. We went ashore and, appropriately, had a Polynesian meal.

So to our last day. We had a final brief sail between 9 am and noon and enjoyed a tacking course to return to base. Packing chores were relieved by a dip in the Sunsail pool. Sunsail took the boat back to its mooring so we had to dinghy back and forth for our taxi to our celebration supper at the Hawaiki NVI Hotel, where lobster thermidor was on the menu. We returned to spend our final night aboard.

The following morning, we were taken from the boat at 7:30. We flew from Raiatea to Tahiti and had the run of the Sofitel Maeve Beach resort at Papeete, for three days including two nights. This was a delightful resort with a palm fringed beach, a swimming pool, enormous beds and where in the evening we watched the sun setting behind the island of Moorea. We took the local open-sided bus into the town and shopped in the market with its huge array of food and souvenirs. On our final evening we were treated to a display of Polynesian dancing; unfortunately, Janet and David missed this as they had an earlier flight to catch. For us it was the perfect ending to our Polynesian adventure.

No life time sailing experience should be complete without a voyage in French Polynesia and, in particular, to Bora Bora with its dramatic volcanic background.

Navigation In Bora-Bora

Reference has been made to voyages which take boats through a pass in a surrounding coral reef into a lagoon which includes a massif at its centre. Bora Bora is a classic example. Since it is possible to circle the massif clockwise or anticlockwise, this can lead to misunderstanding. In theory, this would require two sets of red and green buoys depending on your direction. Mariners should be aware that the buoys placed in these types of islands are coloured on the basis that navigation is being undertaken anticlockwise and that red cylindrical buoys are on the side of the mainland or massif and the green conical buoys are on the reef side.

Welcomed with Traditional Lei garland

Hawaiki Nui Outrigger Canoe Race

Evening at "Bloody Mary's"

Fruit fare offered at the Lagoonarium

Mt Otemanu, Bora Bora

Sarong Demo Sunset over Moorea

Polynesian Dance Performance

Three-Generation Gulet Charter, 2012
Gulf of Gokova, Turkey

This was an ambitious venture bringing 3 generations, separated across the world, to come together in the beautiful cruising ground which is the south coast of Turkey. The size and functionality of a Turkish gulet was ideal for accommodating our issue with their spouses and children plus the parents of Kiwi son-in-law, Elsa and Ron, who joined us from New Zealand.

Our good fortune was to charter a beautiful gulet named "Ulucinar" arranged through an Irish business man who was working with a consortium to build luxury boats on the south coast of Turkey. "Ulucinar" and her crew were magnificent and we could not have been in better hands. The gulet trade is a large component of the Turkish holiday business and the current instability is a massive blow to livelihoods in this area.

So flights wound their way from the UK and New Zealand delivering two sets of grandparents and two family units, one with two boys, Ross aged 4 and Thomas aged 7, and the other with two girls, Zoe aged 8 and Chloe who would celebrate her 12th birthday on board later in the week. We wandered around the marina in Bodrum until we found "Ulucinar"; the children were wide eyed as we boarded this beautiful vessel. This was the start of a magic week.

We were met by the owner's agent who introduced us to the crew which comprised Captain Hussein, crew Ali and Ilderin and cook Ishmael, all of whom were determined to see we had a good time. Little rituals were established up front; spirits were our responsibility but as soon as we placed the gin bottle on the on-deck dining table, the ice and tonic followed immediately. The cook had a portable grill on deck which complemented the freshness of meat, vegetables and fruit which were on offer at every meal. A special meal with cake was also provided for Chloe's birthday. A spacious main cabin provided the chance to read, play games, do crosswords, and ponder over scrabble and the stern cockpit where meals were taken was also furnished with large cushions for relaxing.

It is difficult to do justice to our accommodation. Each of the four adult pairs and both pairs of children had their own en suite cabins with overhead opening lights as well as portholes, all of which presented beautifully.

All aboard, we left the marina and anchored across the bay where following superb catering in the evening with moonlight lighting a path to the ship, we settled down for our first night.

Next morning, up early, we all experienced and enjoyed our first swim. Following breakfast, we cruised eastwards anchoring off Orak Adasi. Here all the toys were launched and great fun was had on the canoes. Ross, fitted with a lifejacket, showed no fear jumping into the 30ft deep turquoise water. We then continued our passage to Cokertme where we dined at Captain Ibrahim's restaurant. This was nostalgic for us having visited here in 1997 on a previous flotilla.

Unfortunately, next morning Ross was running a fever so we were delayed while antibiotics were delivered from Bodrum. This provided the opportunity for some of us to explore the local countryside. Hearing of our previous visit Captain Ibrahim, now in a wheelchair, was brought to meet us. Conditions were now ideal to hoist the sails and we had a relaxing sail across the Gulf to Gerence Buku at the north eastern end of the Datcha Peninsula.

The following morning saw us in a delightful bay east of Gerence Cove. Anchored some distance off, Ali conveyed the families to the wide beach in the tender boat where swimming and canoeing were again the order of the day. Zoe in particular gained in confidence. She decided to swim back to the boat with the aid of her foam float, nicknamed "Toffee". Having reached the boat, she then decided to swim back to the beach, no mean feat for an 8-year-old. Later we transferred to a southern bay inside Yedi Adalari, a chain of seven islands. Again, we had visited here in 1997 but in very different conditions with winds making the sea 'a bit lumpy' as declared by a Yorkshire crew! A wonderful afternoon of water activities ensued with everyone having turns of the Pico dinghy, the windsurfer and the canoes. Finally, we anchored in the northern most bay where we went ashore and enjoyed ice creams.

Next day our destination was Sehir Adalari some 15 nautical miles to the north-east which comprises two islands lying off shore, one named Castle Island and the other Snake Island. We went ashore on Castle Island where we explored the Byzantine ruins including a small amphitheatre situated among olive groves. We enjoyed refreshments, then we walked round to Cleopatra's beach for a swim. Legend has it that Cleopatra arranged to have galley loads of sand shipped from North Africa to create the beach for her lover Anthony. This was a beautiful spot which we shared with Russians on a trip from a hotel on the mainland at the eastern end of the Gulf.

We moved on to Degiren Buku, also known as English Harbour, so called since it hosted a boat station in World War 2. It is an enclosed bay offering all-round shelter. Again, once anchored, the crew launched all the toys for us to enjoy water activities. We then moored across the bay on the quay side where we dined ashore and witnessed a brilliant sunset to complete another enthralling day.

We woke to a beautiful still morning with glassy calm waters and were soon underway motoring passed the statue of a mermaid to starboard. Our passage took us to Alakisla Buku. a small bay with rocky island inhabited by noisy and angry seagulls. That night the families decided to sleep on deck.

10th June, Chloe's 12th birthday; so card and present opening was the first priority of the day. Then we were under way again and the morning passed with on board activities – craft and jewellery making and word games. Our final destination was on the NW side of the island of Gorecik, an anchorage popularly known as "The Aquarium". More swimming fun ensued; Thomas finally plucked up the courage to jump in and swim from the boat and having gained confidence proceeded to circumnavigate the boat twice! The day ended with a birthday meal complete with chocolate cake. We took the opportunity to make a fuss of the crew. Thanks were extended to Captain Hussein for taking us to such great locations, to Ali and Ilderin for looking after us so diligently and launching all boats and canoes whenever we anchored and finally, but not least, to Ishmael for providing splendid meals.

The following morning it was back to Bodrum where the ladies went shopping for traditional goods and souvenirs and the rest of the family enjoyed the facilities of a nearby hotel. Then it was time to say farewell to Elsa and Ron and take our flight home to UK.

In recalling something which was special, one must be careful not to over egg the pudding. Having noted that caution, this was very special and remembered by all as a wonderful family experience.

"Ulucinar"

Fun for all

The expert and the beginner

Splendid fare

Chloe's 12th Birthday

Norfolk Broads Charters

Another influence in the progression to our charter and flotilla voyages was the Norfolk Broads. Reference has been made elsewhere to the advantages of waring round when a tack may cause a problem; this is a common resort on the Broads. Neil was used to this in early school visits to the Broads. These were followed by a week's sailing in 1957 in an engineless boat with brother James, where the principal concern was to protect the crate of Whitbread's in the forepeak, and then in 1967 with Valerie. We nearly did a "Didn't mean to go to sea" (the title of an Arthur Ransome book based on the same waters) going down below Acle on a spring ebb tide without an engine.

Lastly, when in midyears we began to enjoy cycling we took a week in part to cycle in the area and in part to sail. We hired a Bermudan rigged boat out of Martham and enjoyed again the special atmosphere of the Broads. We took a Bermudan rather than a gaff rig forgetting the benefit of the gaff rig being to catch more wind with less heeling. Further, getting a Bermudan mast down to go through the bridge at Potter Heigham was a challenge. At least the water level was low and we did not need to take on passengers to reduce our freeboard to pass under the bridge. Later and perhaps not surprisingly, we came across "Winkle Brig" friends Cynthia and Roger Parish; they were relaxing at Horning but now sailing a Minstrel 23.

A source of great satisfaction was to enjoy the ambience by cycle; the opportunity to visit Ranworth Church and to ascend its tower was particularly memorable as was the visit to the Horsey Mere Windmill. This historic windmill was built to drain water from the dykes and ditches on nearby farmland. It is worth a visit in its own right; the view from the top is special and one can only marvel at the engineering skills of our forebears.

Visiting the Broads is not only a scenic and waterborne experience, it can be a gastronomic one. Hickling Broad lies at one extremity of the area and this should not be missed neither should a visit to "The Pleasure Boat Inn". Likewise,

"The Red Lion" at the head of Thurne Dyke is also worthy of a visit, though to find a berth in the Dyke may be difficult at busy times. Adjacent to the dyke is the handsome Thurne Dyke Windmill, again built for drainage, which we saw in a handsome repainted mode.

Alas, our memories of this idyllic, time warped ambience are now history, since everywhere tempus fugit. Sleepy farm dwellings along the rivers have become elegant holiday retreats, particularly where a small associated inlet allows a boat to be moored. The boat yards at places like Potter Heigham comprise large maintenance buildings servicing a growing hire-craft fleet. The sad aspect is that care and maintenance costs are no more for an eight berth motor boat than they are for a small yacht; the former are now met everywhere one navigates. There is some regard for tradition. The Old Gaffers Society keep and maintain a large fleet of restored traditional gaff rigged boats to which access is available in return for voluntary funds and labour. I would we had more of this kind of attitude in our modern world. One of our favourite photographs of the Broads, which Valerie has reproduced as a water colour, is of three of these craft enjoying a close winded sail. Alas we cannot dwell permanently on nostalgia but must move on to enjoy our sailing as the world would have us.

Traditional gaff rigged boats

WATCH OFFICER, STS SIR WINSTON CHURCHILL
SOUTHAMPTON TO SWANSEA VIA CHERBOURG AND ALDERNEY.
STA VOYAGE NUMBER 184, 3RD TO 16TH JULY 1977. (ADULTS).
MASTER: CAPTAIN R.W. ROWE

Sandwiched between high pressure to the north and low pressure to the south, winds were light and easterly. Progress was slow but sufficient to reach across to Cherbourg and then on to Alderney. The wind freshened here and prudence dictated we left; in fact, we ran before light winds to Torquay and Falmouth. Sadly, after rounding Land's End, winds were still light and we were obliged to motor sail on to Swansea.

Total 746 miles: 26 miles under engine, 129 miles motor-sailing and 591 miles under sail, an average speed of 5kts.

WATCH OFFICER, STS SIR WINSTON CHURCHILL
SOUTHAMPTON TO LONDON VIA CHERBOURG.
STA VOYAGE NUMBER 211, 3RD TO 9TH DECEMBER 1978.
(ADULTS).
MASTER: CAPTAIN J.B. SWINDELLS

We had deep low pressure in the Atlantic to the west of us and high pressure to the east over Scandinavia and southerly gales were expected. We hoped after Cherbourg to have a fair wind up the Channel. Alas the wind came from the east and we were left with no choice but to motor-sail in a SE gale to Dover to catch the flood to take us up to London. Once in the Estuary, we were able to carry square sails as far as Margaret Ness. Our early arrival meant the course members were able to contribute to getting gear ashore before winter refitting.

Total 311 miles: 47 miles under engine, 225 miles motor-sailing and 39miles under sail, an average speed of 6.7 kts.

WATCH OFFICER, STS SIR WINSTON CHURCHILL
SOUTHAMPTON TO LONDON VIA AMSTERDAM.
STA VOYAGE NUMBER 265, 29TH NOV TO 5TH DEC 1981. (ADULTS).
MASTER: CAPTAIN M. KEMMIS-BETTY

A favourable north westerly wind gave us the opportunity to sail off the berth into Southampton Water in boisterous conditions. This favoured us as far as the Royal Sovereign light-house where the wind backed so that we had to turn south to hand the raffee and square topsail. It was then close hauled up to Cap Gris-Nez in the Dover straights. Such were the conditions later gusting to Force 8 that the outer jib and foresail were damaged and handed and there was much mal de mer. The damaged sails were replaced with a storm jib and the main. Then via Rotterdam, Ijmuiden and the rail bridge on the Noordzee canal, we arrived in Amsterdam. Our return to London was motoring into headwinds.

Total 519 miles: Maximum wind speed Force 8.

WATCH OFFICER, STS SIR WINSTON CHURCHILL
SOUTHAMPTON TO PLYMOUTH VIA CHERBOURG.
STA VOYAGE NUMBER. 294, 21ST AUGUST TO 3RD SEPTEMBER 1983
(GIRLS) (TALL SHIPS RACE)
MASTER: CAPTAIN M. KEMMIS-BETTY

A windless start in poor visibility saw us motoring across the Channel to Cherbourg before returning to Weymouth Bay. Since the visibility was still poor, the crew were landed ashore to socialise with other crews prior to racing. After relocating to Portland and more social events, we took part in the Parade of Sail ahead of the race to St Malo. In the race, the "Miller" beat the "Churchill". After the race, with a ferry nearby, the "Miller" altered course to make a pass under the stern of the "Churchill"; unfortunately, she clipped the "Churchill's" stern. At St Malo, socialising continued with the Cutty Sark cocktail party on the "Churchill" and breakfast after a run around the town. After repairs to our bulwark, we made a stormy passage back, sailing into Causand Bay and thence to a berth alongside Trinity Quay.

Total 587 miles: 81 miles under engine, 101 miles motor-sailing & 405 miles under sail, average speed of 4.6kts. Max wind speed Force 6.

WATCH OFFICER, STS SIR WINSTON CHURCHILL
SOUTHAMPTON TO SHOREHAM VIA ST MALO AND CHERBOURG.
STA VOYAGE NUMBER C393A 13TH TO 19th NOVEMBER 1988
(ADULTS) MASTER: CAPTAIN M. FOREWOOD

The voyage got off to a good start there having been a high-pressure area over Europe which was holding. When we eventually put to sea, there was no wind. We had no choice but to motor-sail and chose St Malo as an attractive destination; we drifted for a while awaiting the tide to St Malo. We enjoyed a 24-hour stay. On departure under plain sail we tacked as far as the Minquiers. From the Minquiers we set square sails and enjoyed a good sail through the Alderney Race. Rather than carry on into Lyme Bay we reversed our course and headed back towards Cherbourg. At length, we were able to sail off our berth; we had to rescue the ship's boat with a failed engine. We made a fast passage with downwind sails to St Catherine's Point before bearing away to Shoreham. We moored up for a winter stay.

Total 463 miles: 20 miles under engine, 155 miles motor-sailing and 288 miles under sail, an average speed of 5.3 kts. Max wind speed Force 6/7

WATCH OFFICER, STS MALCOLM MILLER
SOUTHAMPTON TO LONDON VIA AMSTERDAM.
STA VOYAGE NUMBER 258, 21ST TO 27TH 1982. (MIXED ADULTS).
MASTER: CAPTAIN C. BLAKE

From Southampton, we had a fair wind and set topsails and tween mast stay sails. Later as the wind increased, these were handed and we sailed with fore, main and mizzen sails reefed. With a good and fair blow behind us, we were able to sail into the lock at Ijmuiden and then sail up the canal to Amsterdam arriving 1900 hrs. on the Tuesday. Departing 0200 hrs on the following day we motored as far as the breakwaters at Ijmuiden and then set sail. The wind, however, stayed in the south west and increased to force 9 allowing us to maintain a south westerly course past the Smiths Knoll light on the Norfolk coast to the Sunk lightship off Harwich and then up the Thames to our berth on Friday the 25th.

Total 581 miles: 26 miles under engine, 99 miles motor-sailing and 456 miles under sail, an average speed 6.67 kts. Maximum wind speed Force 9.

WATCH OFFICER, STS MALCOLM MILLER
SOUTHAMPTON TO SHOREHAM VIA CHERBOURG AND HONFLEUR
STA VOYAGE NUMBER. M329(A) 30TH NOV TO 6TH DEC 1986
(ADULTS)
MASTER: CAPTAIN A.J.N. ALLENBY

We departed at 0800 hrs in the wake of the "Sir Winston Churchill". Past the Brambles Bank, sails were set in a south westerly blow force 6 to 7 and a lumpy sea. Reefs were required and the motion was then more comfortable overnight ahead of arrival at Cherbourg the following afternoon. After French delicacies ashore we went back to sea overnight en route to Honfleur. Honfleur is an attractive place to be and we also enjoyed fine weather here and a nice evening meal ashore. The next day saw us departing at 1000 hrs into a blustery S.S.W. Force 8 which gave us a fairly swift passage back to Shoreham but not able to arrive until after high tide. Even the following day, we had winds gusting up to 45 knots and the pilot had a problem getting on board. With the pilot on board, we managed to feel our way into Shoreham Harbour and our refit berth.

Total 378 miles: 43 miles under engine, 62 miles motor-sailing and 273 miles under sail, an average speed of 5.4 kts. Max wind speed Force 8

WATCH OFFICER, STS MALCOLM MILLER
SOUTHAMPTON TO SHOREHAM VIA ST MALO
STA VOYAGE NO. M393 19TH TO 25TH NOVEMBER 1989 (ADULTS).
MASTER: CAPTAIN A.J.N. ALLENBY

There was a frustrating start into little wind dictating motoring down to the Needles where sails were set and tack and gybe routines rehearsed. Again we had to resort to motor sailing as we approached the Alderney race with the Minquiers beyond en route to St Malo. St Malo lock was open until 1400 hrs and we just made it. After a run ashore, getting the bow off the quay with a strong onshore wind gusting to 20 kts. was a challenge. We had a fast passage up through the race but then had to motor sail across the Channel. Overnight we were close hauled along the coast towards Shoreham. After a boat trip to take photos, early evening found us anchored off Shoreham. The crew laid on a Xmas Dinner after which we entered the locks and made our way to the refit berth.

Total 419 miles: 42 miles under engine, 181 miles motor-sailing and 196 miles under sail, an average speed of 5.11 kts. Max wind speed Force 6

DECK HAND, STS "STAVROS NIARCHOS"
GREENOCK TO SWANSEA VIA DUBLIN
VOYAGE NUMBER SSN584, 9TH TO 15TH MAY 2013 (ADULTS).
MASTER: CAPTAIN RADEK EVANS

To sail as a deckhand on the "Stavros Niarchos" was a very different experience to sailing as a Watch Officer in the STA ships. I was now in my 73rd year – to the rest of the crew I was "old" and had to work at being considered useful and sociable. One way was to be prepared to climb into the rigging, respond to commands and to communicate.

For me the voyage started with high emotion passing my beloved Kyles of Bute. Our journey to Dublin was uneventful and we entered the River Liffey in company with a Stena Line vessel. Once through the lifting bridge we docked just short of the new cable stayed bridge (the "Jeannie Johnstone" coffin ship replica was just the other side of the bridge on the opposite bank). A visit to a Dublin pub on a Saturday evening was pure joy; we seemed to be the only ones present without our own musical instruments!

Swansea bound the following day, we had a fair wind kicking up a moderate sea. Our bearing allowed us to carry a square course with both upper and lower topsails on the foremast and above the main we had a lower top sail. It was a great sail under the South Bishop Light in its dramatic setting. I shed tears of nostalgia as we passed Skomer Island, Milford Haven and Stackpole Quay where my family learned the joy of sailing together. Then so to Swansea where I was met by Valerie who enjoyed a visit to the ship.

Total Mileage 395: 267 miles under engine, 128 miles under sail.

Maximum wind speed Force 7

The "Stavros Niarchos" has been sold away. It is a crying shame that vessels and opportunities like this are now denied to our young people and to those still young at heart.

Valerie and I hope our message reaches the right ears.

The Joys of Being Afloat

Sailing cannot be divorced from the sensation of being afloat. Conversely there are lots of stimulating opportunities to be afloat which don't involve sailing. We have enjoyed a number of these.

Africa, Cape Town excepted, does not offer many sailing opportunities but perversely offers some diverse methods of getting afloat. One of these is the Victoria Falls in the dry season. Most people visit the falls in the wet season since the water cascading down is more dramatic. Against this is the view of the falls can be spoiled by a dense mist. In the dry season, the falls are not as dramatic but this allows access to small lakes which lie immediately behind the falls' cliff edge. With a local guide hanging on to your ankles, you can actually extend your head over the vertical wall and see the water cascading down on to the rocks and pools below. Floating doesn't get much better than this. As to the falls they are impressive, but pale into insignificance compared with South America's Iguazu Falls.

We have referred earlier to colonial times afloat where British penetration into South Africa was via the east coast through Knysna and Cape Town. Knysna is far from a safe anchorage but it had to do. We were able to get afloat as far as the enclosing headlands in Knysna using the local tourist boat. Similarly, the Germans were trying to colonise West Africa from the even more hostile "Skeleton Coast" off Namibia using the port of Swakopmund which was no more secure than Knysna. Again we had the opportunity to take a tourist catamaran trip out across the shallow water off Swakopmund.

Sailing has always been about horses for courses and the underwater profile on which the boat floats. This has local implications and one which is very evident is the choice of rig to sail in Chesapeake Bay. Chesapeake Bay boasts a large area in which to sail and has waterside ambience and history to go with it. It has one drawback; it is relatively shallow. This dictates the preferred rig which is either the yawl, with the mizzen set aft of the rudder, or the schooner. In both rigs the sail is spread along the hull rather than high above the deck. In relatively calm conditions, a "Frenchie" (a small square shaped fore and aft sail) can be carried at the forward mast head; I had not seen this before but recognised its functionality. The other attraction of Chesapeake is that it links up with the US Naval Academy.

A cruise liner is the epitome of elegant and relaxing floating. It is, of course, much more than this since it takes in the history of where you happen to be and how the scenery presents along the way. We enjoyed a passage from Barbados to New York aboard the QM2; you can't fault the ship other than while exploring on board you run into signs which say "1st Class Only". The classiest thing on board was a Maritime Library which would stand comparison with libraries in the capital cities of Maritime Nations. However, the highlight was taking a catamaran excursion from the ship into St Lucia and we marvelled at the spectacle of The Pitons. Also, a similar excursion in the British Virgin Islands, brought back memories of our earlier flotilla holiday in that area. A self-evident modern phenomenon is the larger the vessel and the older the passengers, the longer it takes to disembark. Beware also the Cruise Liner's trips which are often a substitute for better shore-based facilities. We once watched cruise liner passengers being bused to see the little mermaid in Copenhagen. The mermaid was about 100 yards down the quay!

Another float with a surprising outcome was while lying on an airbed in the pool of a hotel in Death Valley. This is of no significance until you connect it with the fact that you have also floated in a reed boat on Lake Titicaca. The connection between the two is the vertical distance between them. Apparently if you want to claim the world vertical floating record, currently held by Tristan Jones who wrote a book about it, you have to go and float in the Dead Sea.

We have done some more floating which is often described as messing around in boats. On holiday in California we looked at a map with a UK sense of distance and observed that this place Hawaii lay just off the west coast. Several hours and expensive flights later we found ourselves on a beach at Waikiki floating on a surf board. We also dined in a restaurant one side of which was a large aquatic tank which contained not only exotic coloured fish but also a young lady with not a lot on feeding the fish.

In Bangkok we experienced a unique way of floating, namely on a ferry powered by a bus engine. These relatively small punt shaped boats mounted a large bus engine amidships at an incline so that the prop shaft was a direct drive to the propeller at the stern. Efficiency gone mad; I have only once seen a similar arrangement in the UK.

America's Cup Boats are accessible and "New Zealand 2" was in Auckland Harbour when we were visiting our son-in-law's folks. We were welcomed on board and we actually went for a sail. Before this we were briefed on winch handling. It was explained that different winches do different tasks and we were then asked to complete the task, i.e. one group to hoist a head sail and another group to hoist the mainsail. We laboured to no avail. They then explained that below decks, every winch can be geared to any function; we were winching against one another! To add insult to injury, my duty was to stow the spinnaker in the forepeak as it was taken down. I felt relieved when they realised I was still there buried under acres of canvas. In Sydney, we could not access an America's Cup boat but we were able to get afloat with an old ex-pat financial pal who had ended up with a beautiful harbourside home at Mosman. He had a motor cruiser which he kept afloat at the bottom of the garden. After a trip around Sydney Harbour, he took us for lunch at the Royal Squadron Yacht Club; where else would you go if you live at Mosman!

Another source of great satisfaction is being afloat on the UK canal system. We enjoyed a long-term friendship with Valerie's friend Caroline who, together with husband Chris, invited us to join them on their boat on two of the "must do" UK stretches. These are the Black Country Ring and the Llangollen Canal.

The Black Country Ring was very nostalgic for Neil since it starts in the centre of Birmingham, the city of his birth, and runs northwest past all the forges and foundries which were part of his training to become a metallurgist. Both Birmingham, in Gas St Basin, and Wolverhampton have facilities for boats passing through. On our second trip we travelled up the delightful Shropshire Union canal to reach the Llangollen Canal. The more remote the canal became, the more we saw mature boats being used as houseboats. Their self-sufficiency extended to growing produce in pots on the decks and roofs; we did spy the odd cannabis root amongst them. The highlight of the Llangollen Canal is the Pontcysyllte Aqueduct which carries the canal over the river Dee. It stands 38m above the river. Taking a boat across the aqueduct is quite nerve racking. I got to helm; the boat owner Chris suffered from vertigo.

Viaducts and Bridges are always diverting while afloat. Our brig launch to the Festival at Edinburgh was under the loom of the Forth Rail bridge and as described in our voyage to Florida, the bridge crossing Tampa bay at the head of the Intracoastal waterway was impressive. We were also taken by friends for a sail out under the Golden Gate Bridge in San Francisco which looks dramatic from the deck of a small yacht. The cruising ground immediately beyond the bridge is not very welcoming.

The canals in South Wales are also worth exploring. They played a great part in the enormous wealth which was created by the coal and iron barons who shipped these products down to the dock yards on the south coast. Some of the sailors who shipped the product were Italian Somalis (Italy had colonised part of Somalia). To this day there is a Somali community in Cardiff. The castle at Cardiff ended up in the hands of the Marquis of Bute who developed the coal trade. Other families who benefited were the Morgan and Cory families. All altered the landscape of South Wales with their building projects. The Butes enhanced Cardiff Castle, the Morgans built Tredegar House and the Corys developed Dyffryn House. The latter two also have spacious grounds and formal gardens. We visit both these sites regularly. The coal and iron floated down to the docks and across the sea. The money floated back in return.

A caution; sailing, i.e. floating around waiting for the wind to blow or alternatively trying to remain in control when the wind does blow, is a barrier to remaining financially afloat. Anti-fouling paint is scheduled to be the next hedge against inflation!

"Floating" on the edge of Victoria Falls

Reed boat Lake Titicaca, Peru

Valerie helming America's Cup Yacht "NZL40"

Crossing the aqueduct on Llangollen Canal

Golden Gate Bridge, San Francisco

Pearls from Our Mudbanks

Reef before you broach rather than reefing after you have broached. Always reef early.

Always buoy your anchor.

When swimming ashore with a line, swim ashore with a light line and pull a heavier one after you.

Make sure you can release loaded headsail sheets or you will trap a sail "aback" when you tack.

Make sure your chain is marked so you know how much chain is out.

When you take a bearing, make sure it is on an inanimate object.

If under engine in a windy and crowded anchorage, steer astern. Your engine and tiller are stern thrusters which aid steering and your mast has no option but to follow your stern.

If you are sailing in the lee of a headland, be ready for the change in wind speed as you leave the lee.

Can you find your windlass trip switch in the dark?

Don't follow a radio bearing in a fog; someone else will be doing the same.

Make sure the windlass gypsy is not worn. If it is, steepen the angle at which the chain enters the gypsy. Be careful if you are using your foot. I've seen this done with a bare foot.

Don't use an overweight anchor and chain to anchor your boat in deep water. These factors increase the current to the windlass which may shorten its life. Always have plenty of engine revs when lifting the chain. Do not allow the windlass to tow the boat. Lift continuously rather than intermittently.

When steering through traffic, use sound signals to indicate your change in course.

If he's bigger than you in a harbour with restricted space, he may have difficulty in giving way.

Beware beautiful sunsets at the tops of high mountains. They are often pre-cursers to katabatic winds.

If you can't see a vessel approaching you round a blind bend and therefore you do not know his or your intentions, give a single prolonged blast signal.

Set your SATNAV to the optimum satellites. We once sailed with a SATNAV which happily showed us rounding a headland on the yellow bit rather than the blue bit.

When moored to a quay by stern lines, bear in mind that the stern lines will stretch in a hard gust astern. After the gust, they will act like elastic bands and will exert enough force to propel the vessel toward the quay. There is often too much elasticity in the bow line to prevent this. Use appropriate fenders or, .in a gale, man your engine to keep off the quay.

If your anchor is foul under a cable on the sea bed, see if you can determine the location the cable is coming ashore. Having located this, loop a bight under the cable and, using a dinghy, tow the bight to the stern of the boat. The cable can often be lifted to allow the anchor flukes to be dropped free of the cable.

Don't sail close hauled too close to a cliff coast. Backwinding will disrupt your progress.

If you are steering a line of sight course to a mark, bear in mind your compass bearing may alter due to your being set down wind or down tide.

In fast flowing shallow water, the deepest water is to be found where the flotsam travels fastest.

Legacy Flotilla
Southern Ionian, Greece, 2019

This was a flotilla which we had planned in our dreams for many years and finally the opportunity to pursue it had arrived. We had earlier carried out a gulet charter (see Contents) where we had three generations on board comprising our two daughter's families, one with two sons and one with two daughters, and two sets of grandparents ourselves and son-in-law Chris's parents from New Zealand.

Grandsons, Thomas aged 14 and Ross aged 11, were considered as now meriting a berth on a flotilla boat on the basis that they were older than their mother was when she experienced her first flotilla, and also that they possessed their RYA Level One Certificates. Ross was not content with the one obligatory capsize during his test; he did four just for the hell of it, quote, 'It was great!'

And so we were off, Nan and Gramps, Mum and Dad and the two boys. We chose as our charter company Sailing Holidays with whom we had not sailed previously. The promotion of the flotilla and supporting documents were first class and included considerable detail both with regard to boats and to the sailing area. We selected a one-week flotilla in the Southern Ionian on the basis that the area was familiar to us and that the itinerary appealed. Alas the delivery of the flotilla was not so successful and led to some frustrations. More of this anon.

After the usual hilly trip from Preveza airport to Sivota on the island of Levkas with its bustling if somewhat sprawling waterfront, we were allocated and introduced to our boats. In our case this was a brand new Beneteau 38, "Othoni", boasting a forecabin, more like a stateroom, and two quarter cabins. The former was high-jacked by the boys while the adults squeezed into port and starboard quarter cabins constrained by the hull shape. You sacrificed boat space for 8 knots of speed on a zephyr beam reach. Our day ended with a nostalgic visit to Delphini Taverna, which we had last visited in 1985 when it was then known as Yanni's Taverna. Yanni still runs the Taverna and we had a conversation with him about those early days.

Boat and daily briefing behind us we were underway. Our course lay west of Meganisi Island stopping en route at a bay on the north east corner of N. Thilia Island and then along the north coast of Meganisi to "Little" Vahti. This was a delightful place with the opportunity to be stern-to a quay with but a short walk to the delights of "Stavros" restaurant.

Next day, after a great broad reach sail across the four-pronged headland to the north east of Meganisi, we anchored in the central bay of Abelike for lunch, swimming and paddle board fun. This place is a delight and invokes fond memories of our earlier visits. Then it was a northerly passage to Nidri with ample opportunity for the boys to hone their seamanship en route. Each took a turn at helming and had to don the "Captain's" hat! Nidri has not maintained its old local charm and now has boats anchored or ashore wherever space allowed. The incentives for our visit were a swimming pool ashore and a shore-based BBQ, poor recompense for the distance travelled.

One has to know one Vahti from another. The next day took us to "Big" Vahti on the island of Ithaca; it is the island's capital with facilities to match. It was a long passage and involved retracing our steps down the Meganisi Channel – frustrating. Our frustration was tempered by a visit to a pleasant swimming beach when we reached our destination. After a delicious meal at Dimitri's taverna we took the 20-minute walk into the main town which blends some sophistication with an old-world charm. Our overnight mooring was alongside the North Quay and unfortunately, we found ourselves with a sister flotilla being rafted up to the same quay outside of us.

Due to this we were unable to get away until 11 am the following morning and all haste was made to ensure that we arrived at our next destination, Frikes, by 2:30 pm. as requested. This rather limited the opportunity for a swim and paddle board break. Frikes lies on the north east coast of Ithaca and is a small but pleasant place. Like many communities in these parts it has windmills on adjacent cliffs which provide waymarks and it is worth while taking a walk up to a windmill for the great views. Once again we were rafted up alongside the main quay.

After being kept waiting for our morning briefing, we set off for our next port of call, Vasiliki, which lies at the south end of Levkas Island. Sadly, we did not have time to visit Atokos Island, nicknamed "Donkey" island on a previous visit when we had to ensure the lone donkey was well watered. However, we took time out at the head of the bay of Ammousa where, in company with other boats, we were able to anchor close enough to the shore to run the toys, paddle boards and dinghies, on to a rock fringed shingle beach. Ross's skills at paddle boarding were now so developed that he was able to do a head stand on the board! After a pleasant day's activities in this south coast bay, we had a great sail north to Vasiliki. The harbour and town of Vasiliki lies in the north east corner of a large south facing bay well protected from the prevailing wind from the north. However, it is open to southerly winds. Vasiliki was a delightful place for the various crews to socialise and to be coerced into Greek dancing together.

On our last day we made a short hop to Rouda Beach for a final swim and paddle board session before returning to base at Sivota. Here we dined together with the crew; there was merriment as various incidents along the way were recalled and awards and trophies distributed. All the kids dined on a separate table and then became feral, dashing madly in one direction only to reappear a short time later going in the opposite direction. They eventually settled for international football being widely screened. Sadly, then it was time to pack for our return home.

Being held in school holidays, the lead crew had a difficult job with a flotilla comprising many youngsters and busy traffic afloat and maybe this led the lead crew to be over cautious. Our feedback is when there are difficult and inconvenient decisions to be made like arriving somewhere at 2.30 pm when you don't get away until 11 am, the reasons which give rise to this must be explained. Particularly irksome was being taken to the untidy waterfront which is now Nidri, on the basis there was a local swimming pool ashore and that this was a more convenient place than a beach to hold a BBQ, and then to have to retrace our steps. In fact, the itinerary bore little resemblance to the one we had specially chosen with opportunities to visit old favourites, for example Kastos and Kalamos, denied. Despite the disappointment over the itinerary, for us the flotilla was a success in that our grandsons had a great time and it fulfilled our desire to see them have a flotilla experience. It is interesting to note that there were four other yachts crewed by 3 generations.

Thomas and Ross with RYA Certificates

Ross at the helm   Thomas at the helm

Ross' paddle board head stand

Bibliography (Inspirational)
Neil and Valerie's Library

Yachtsmen spend too much time dreaming instead of doing practical things like working, earning and house maintenance. The next fantasy is inspired by the antics of those who have overcome the burdens of inertia and have set off on extraordinary adventures. Take your pick and while away a winter's evening in the company of the following:

MAIDEN, *Tracy Edwards and Tim Madge*, a 27-year-old takes an all-female crew around the world, Simon and Schuster, 1990

ISLAND RACE, *John McCarthy and Sandi Toksvig*, two novice sailors take an 80-year-old boat around the U.K., BBC 1995

THE CHALLENGE, *Chay Blyth and Elaine Thompson*, 10 67ft steel yachts go around the world in 9 months, Hodder and Stoughton Ltd., 1993

THE LONELIEST RACE, *Paul Gelder.* BOC Challenge 1994-95, Adlard Coles Nautical, 1995

THEN WE SAILED AWAY, *John, Marie, Christine and Rebecca Ridgway*, Circumnavigation of South America via Antarctica, Little, Brown and Co. 1996

THE CHINA VOYAGE, *Tim Severin*, across the Pacific on a bamboo raft, Little Brown and Co. 1994

GIPSY MOTH CIRCLES THE WORLD, *Sir Francis Chichester*, single-handed voyage around the world, Hodder and Stoughton Ltd., 1967

FASTNET FORCE 10, *John Rousmaniere*, the infamous Fastnet race of 1979 during which 15 lives were lost, Nautical Publishing Co Ltd, 1980.

THE SAILING CRUISER, *W.M. Nixon*, the essentials of a sailing cruiser, Nautical Publishing Co. Ltd,1977

SIR PETER BLAKE, AN AMAZING LIFE, *Authorised Biography, Alan Sefton*, Penguin Books, 2006

THE LONELY SEA AND THE SKY, *Francis Chichester*, Hodder and Stoughton, 1964

COME HELL OR HIGH WATER, *Clare Francis*, Royal Western/Observer Single-Handed Transatlantic Race 1976, Pelham Books, 1977. (signed copy)

CRUISING UNDER SAIL, *Eric Hiscock*, a lifetime of sailing experience. Adlard Coles, 1990

THE INCREDIBLE VOYAGE, *Tristan Jones*, Sheridan House, 1977

OVER THE TOP, *Adrian Flanagan*, vertical circumnavigation via Cape Horn and Vil'kitskiy Strait, Weidenfeld and Nicolson 2008.

CRUISING ASSOCIATION HANDBOOK supported by RYA and Forward Trust, Cruising Association, 1971

STANFORD'S SAILING COMPANION, *Captain R.J.F. Riley and Captain F.S. Campbell*, Stanford Maritime Ltd, 1976

RACE AGAINST TIME, *Ellen MacArthur*, solo circumnavigation in catamaran "B&Q", Penguin Non-Fiction, 2006

WHEN I PUT TO SEA, *Nicolette Milnes-Walker*, solo transatlantic crossing, Macmillan, 1973

PASSAGE TO JUNEAU, A SEA & ITS MEANINGS, *Jonathan Raban*, Picador, 1999.

A journey through the above bibliography is a big ask; you may be able to glean an overall feeling of mankind's adventure in sailing boats from Mike Bender's recent book "A New History of Yachting" published by Boydell Press, 2017. It has a foreword by Tom Cunliffe. Likewise, Brian Lavery has recently followed up his earlier book "Empire of the Seas" (written to accompany the BBC series presented by Dan Snow which detailed how the Royal Navy forged the modern world) with a further perspective entitled "Ship, 5000 Years of Maritime Adventure" published by Dorling Kindersley, 2017.

Acknowledgements

The description of our visits to French Polynesia and the Seychelles could not have been produced without access to Janet Dick's travel journal which includes vastly more detail than has been covered in these respective sections. Valerie and Neil are indebted to Janet for her contribution to these voyage reports.

We should also like to thank those who have been brave enough to join us and who have provided us with such precious memories. May it be a long time before your tide sets.

Pat and Geoff Holloway

The Dicks, the Abbotts and the Cookes

The Briggers

Our Wheel of Experiences was put together to provide a record of our exploits

Our Wheel of Experiences